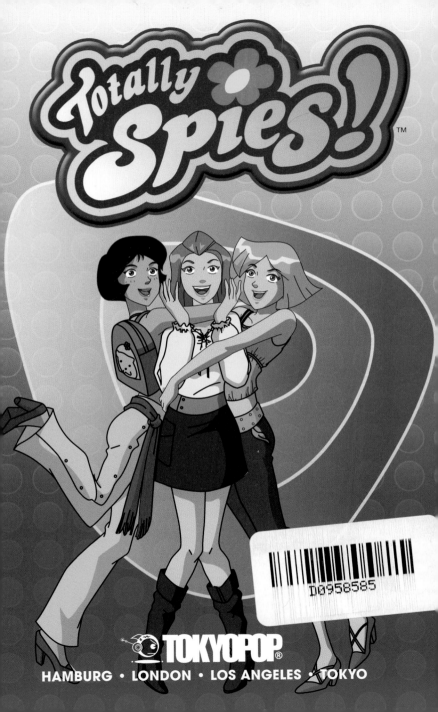

Totally Spies!™

TOKYOPOP®

HAMBURG • LONDON • LOS ANGELES • TOKYO

Editor - Erin Stein
Contributing Editor - Ian Mayer
Graphic Designer and Letterer - Chris Tjalsma
Cover Designers - Tomás Montalvo-Lagos and Anna Kernbaum
Graphic Artists - Louis Csontos and Tomás Montalvo-Lagos

Digital Imaging Manager - Chris Buford
Production Managers - Jennifer Miller and Mutsumi Miyazaki
Senior Designer - Anna Kernbaum
Art Director - Matt Alford
Senior Editor - Elizabeth Hurchalla
Managing Editor - Jill Freshney
VP of Production - Ron Klamert
Editor-in-Chief - Mike Kiley
President & C.O.O. - John Parker
Publisher & C.E.O. - Stuart Levy

E-mail: info@tokyopop.com
Come visit us online at www.TOKYOPOP.com

A **TOKYOPOP** Cine-Manga® Book
TOKYOPOP Inc.
5900 Wilshire Blvd., Suite 2000
Los Angeles, CA 90036

Totally Spies!: Time Spies When You're Having Fun

Series Created by David Michel and Vincent Chalvon-Demersay
Story written by Liz Tigelaar and Holly Henderson

ISBN: 1-59532-818-1

First TOKYOPOP® printing: October 2005

10 9 8 7 6 5 4 3 2 1

Printed in the USA

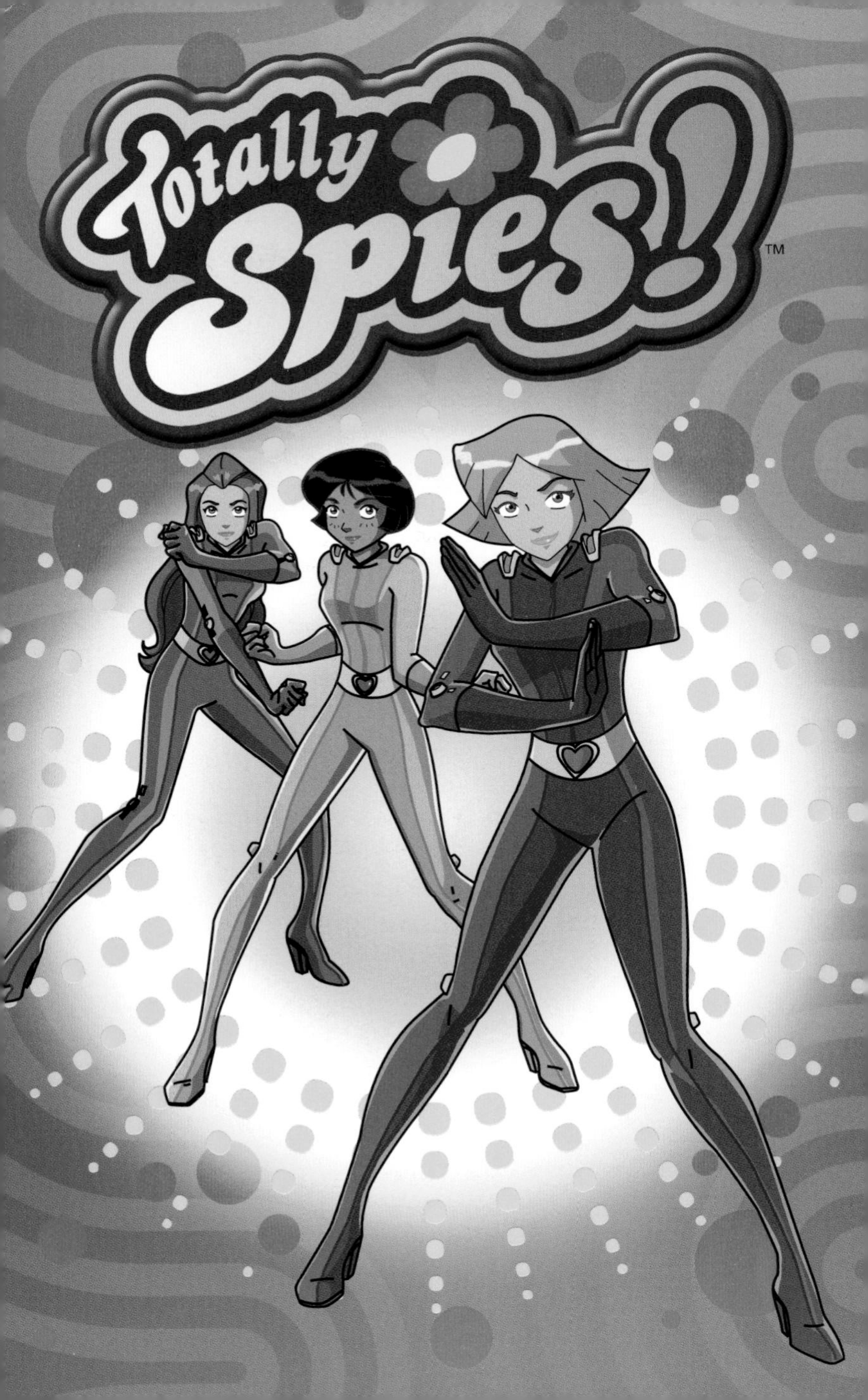
Totally Spies!™

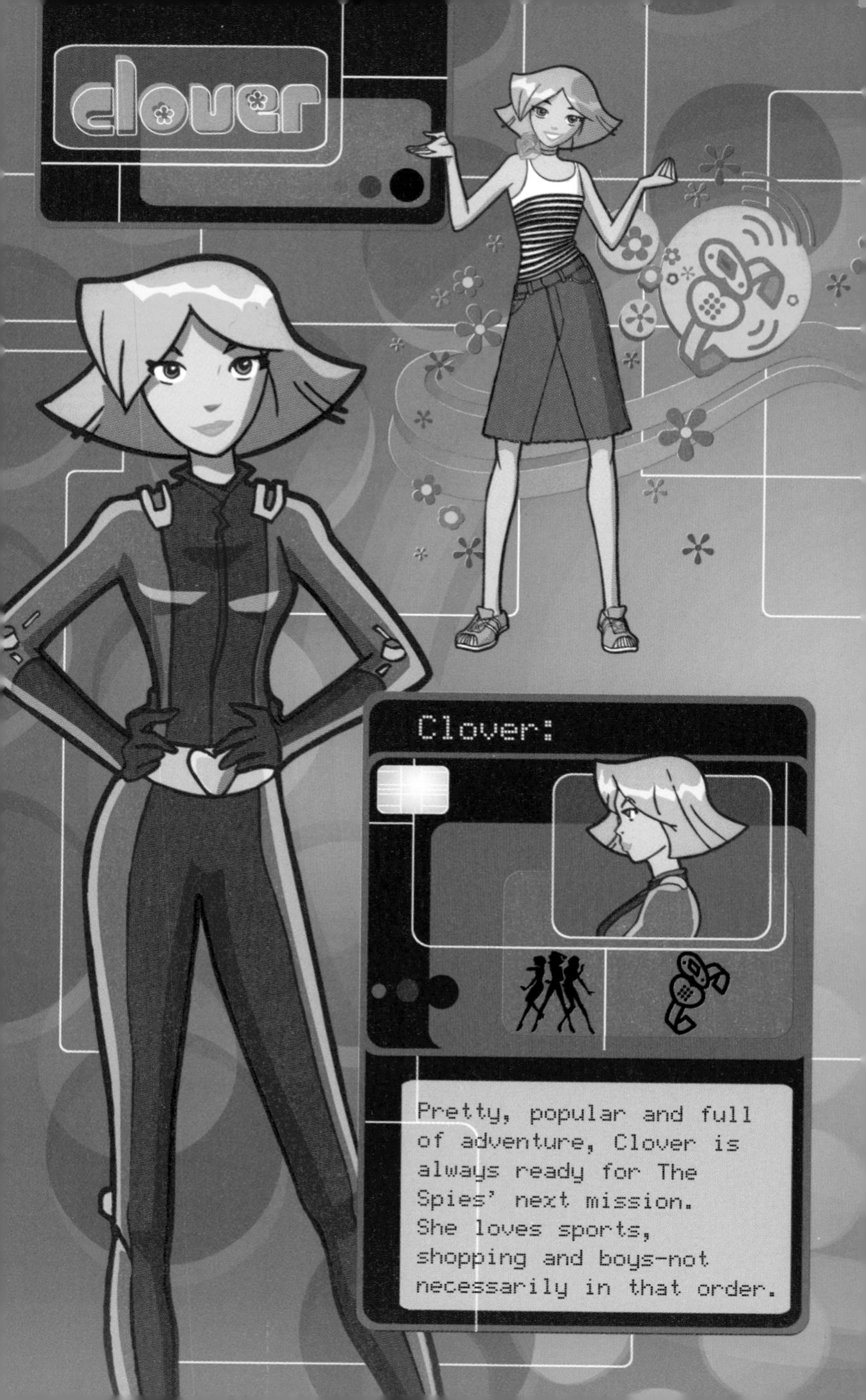
clover
Clover:
Pretty, popular and full of adventure, Clover is always ready for The Spies' next mission. She loves sports, shopping and boys-not necessarily in that order.

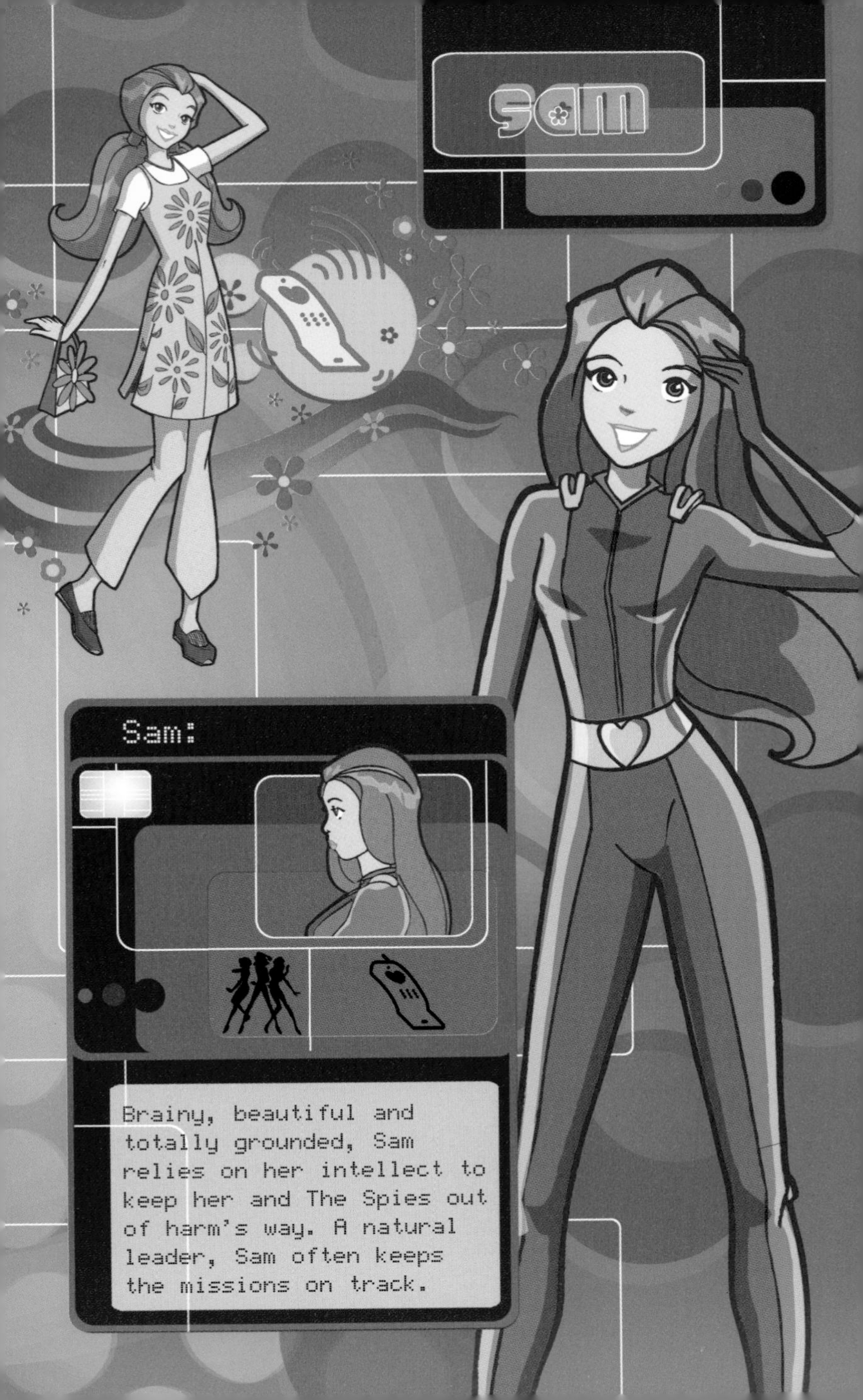
sam
Sam:
Brainy, beautiful and totally grounded, Sam relies on her intellect to keep her and The Spies out of harm's way. A natural leader, Sam often keeps the missions on track.

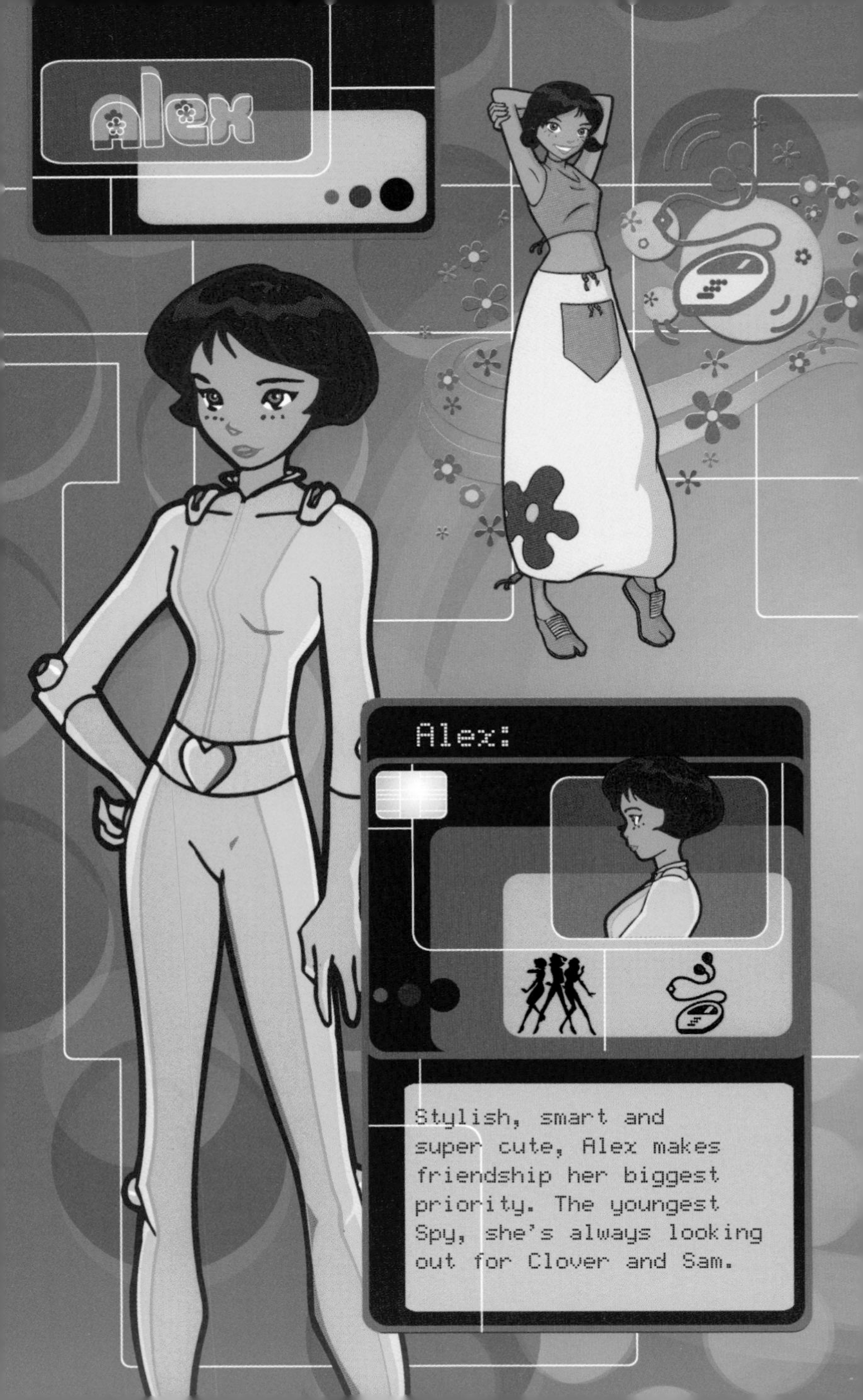
alex
Alex:
Stylish, smart and super cute, Alex makes friendship her biggest priority. The youngest Spy, she's always looking out for Clover and Sam.

Jerry:

The Spies' contact at WOOHP, the World Organization of Human Protection.

Mandy:

The most popular girl at Beverly Hills High.

The Horseman:

A mysterious bad guy who's traveling through time to steal stuff.

The King:

A hunky ruler the girls meet back in time.

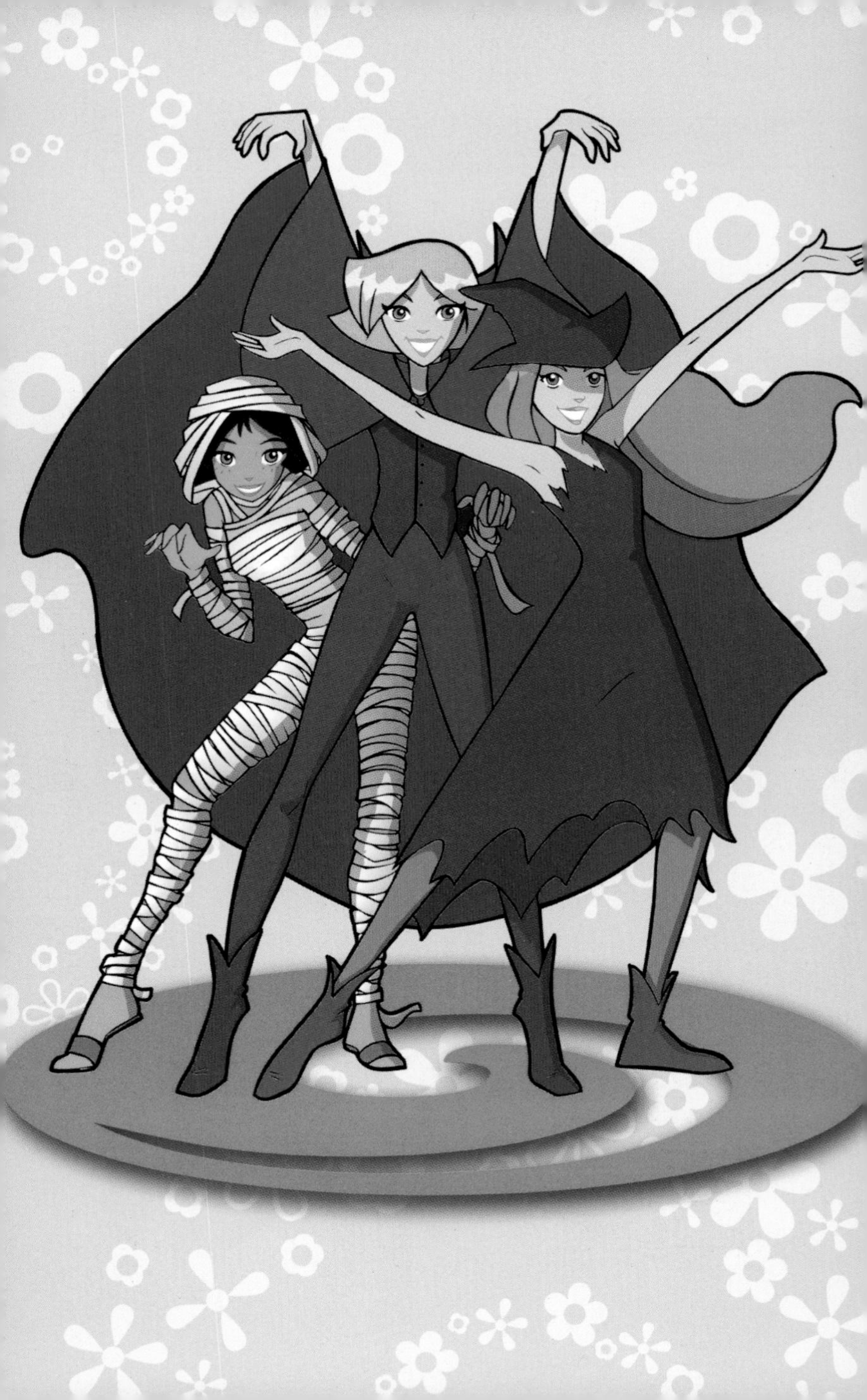

Totally Spies!™

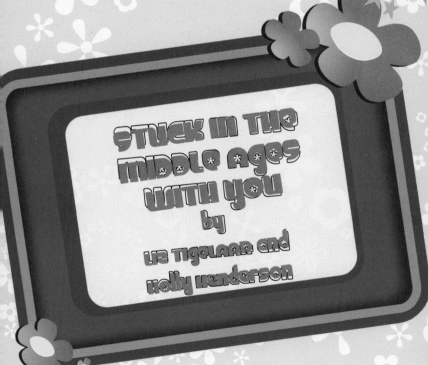

Stuck in the
Middle Ages
with you
by
Liz Tigelaar and
Holly Henderson

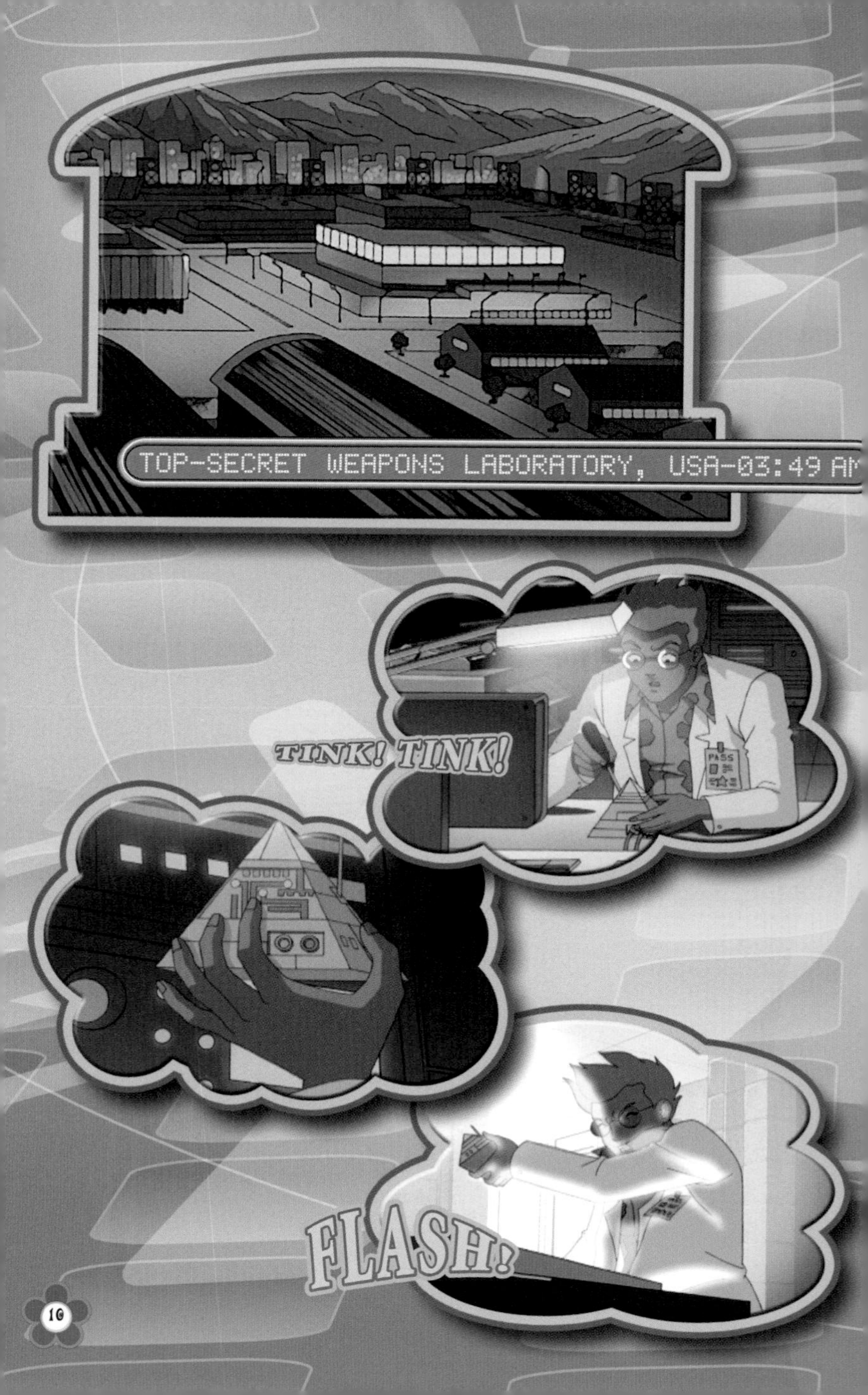
TOP-SECRET WEAPONS LABORATORY, USA-03:49 AM
TINK! TINK!
FLASH!

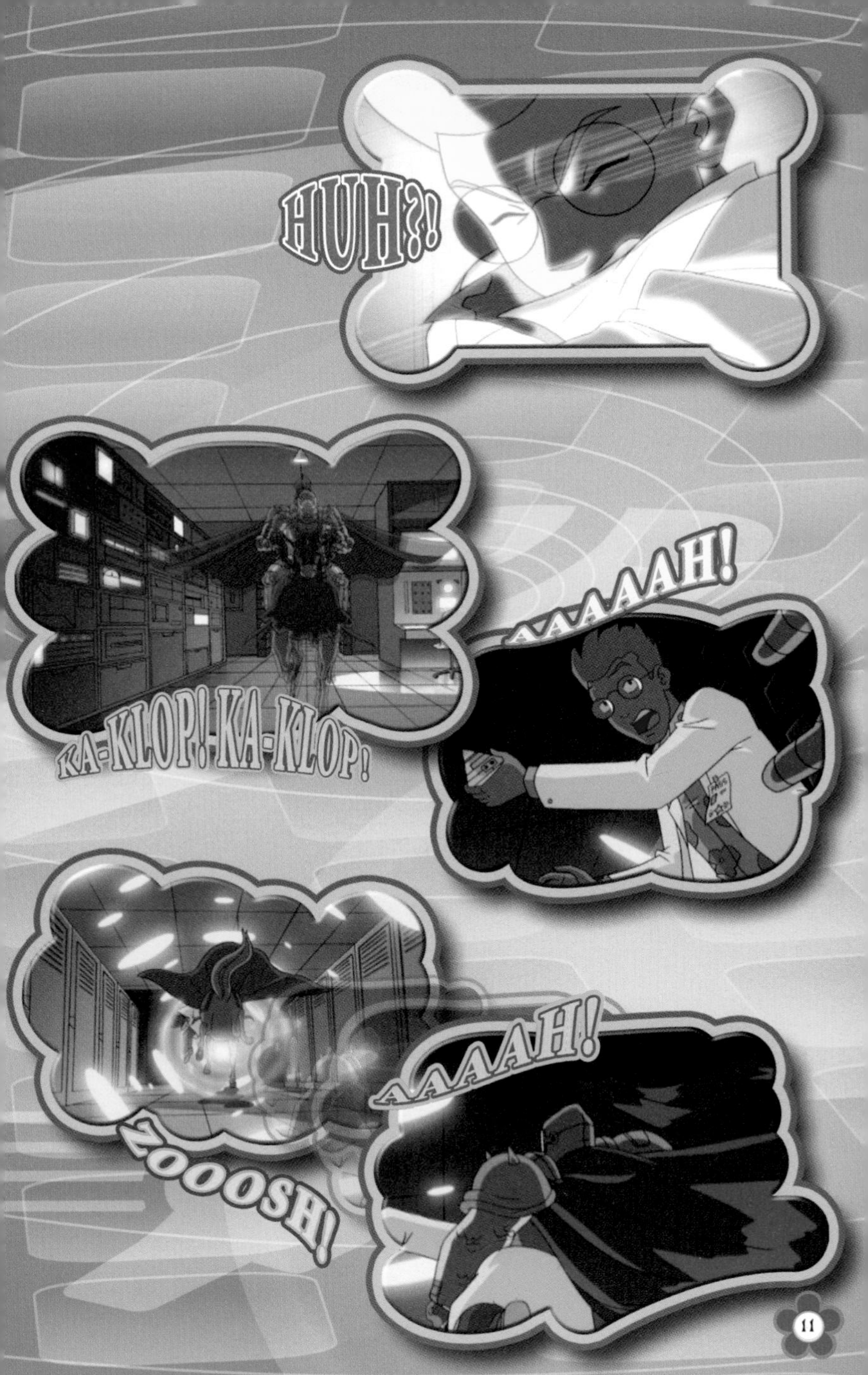
HUH?!
KA-KLOP! KA-KLOP!
AAAAAAH!
ZOOOSH!
AAAAH!

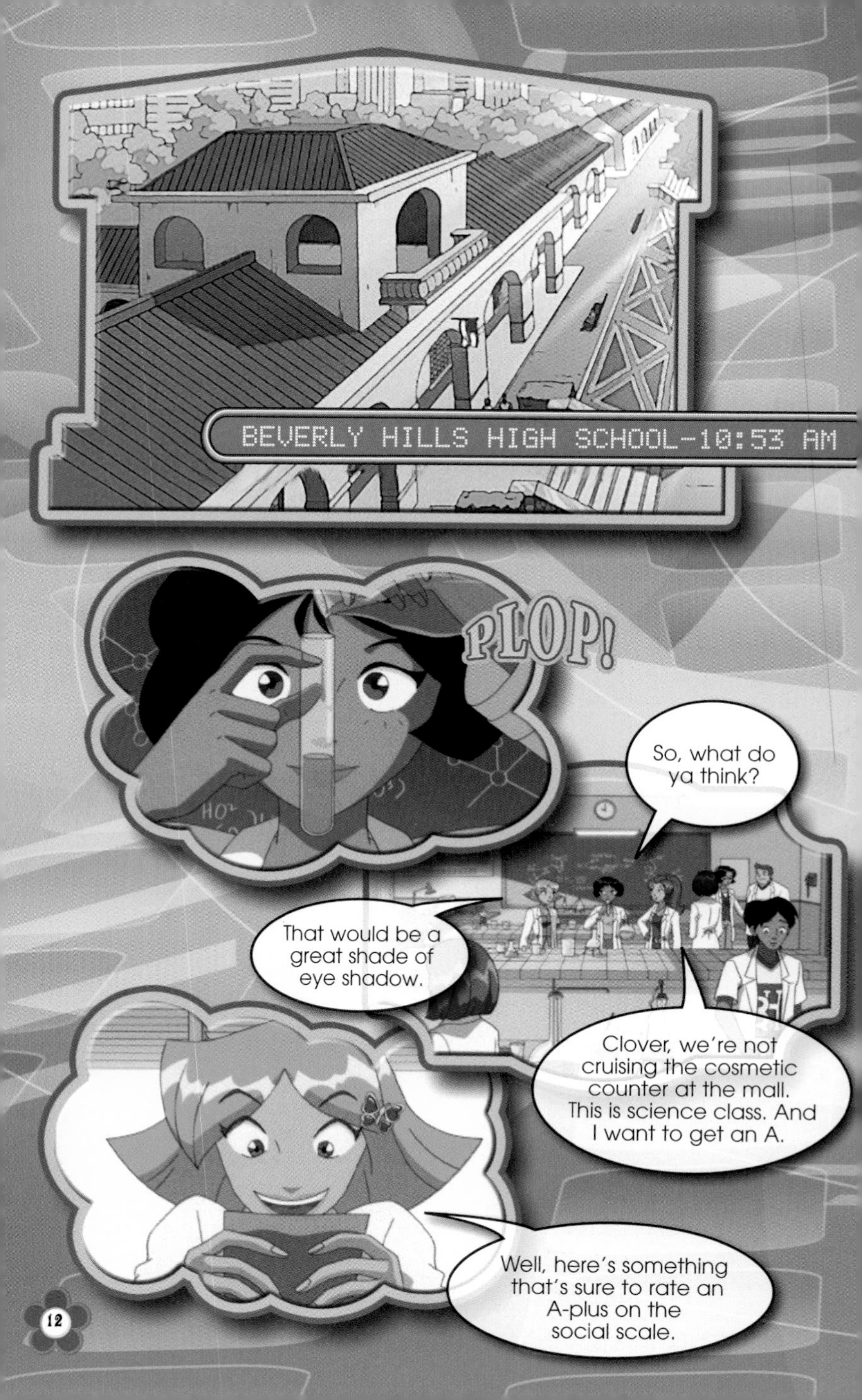
BEVERLY HILLS HIGH SCHOOL-10:53 AM
PLOP!
So, what do ya think?
That would be a great shade of eye shadow.
Clover, we're not cruising the cosmetic counter at the mall. This is science class. And I want to get an A.
Well, here's something that's sure to rate an A-plus on the social scale.

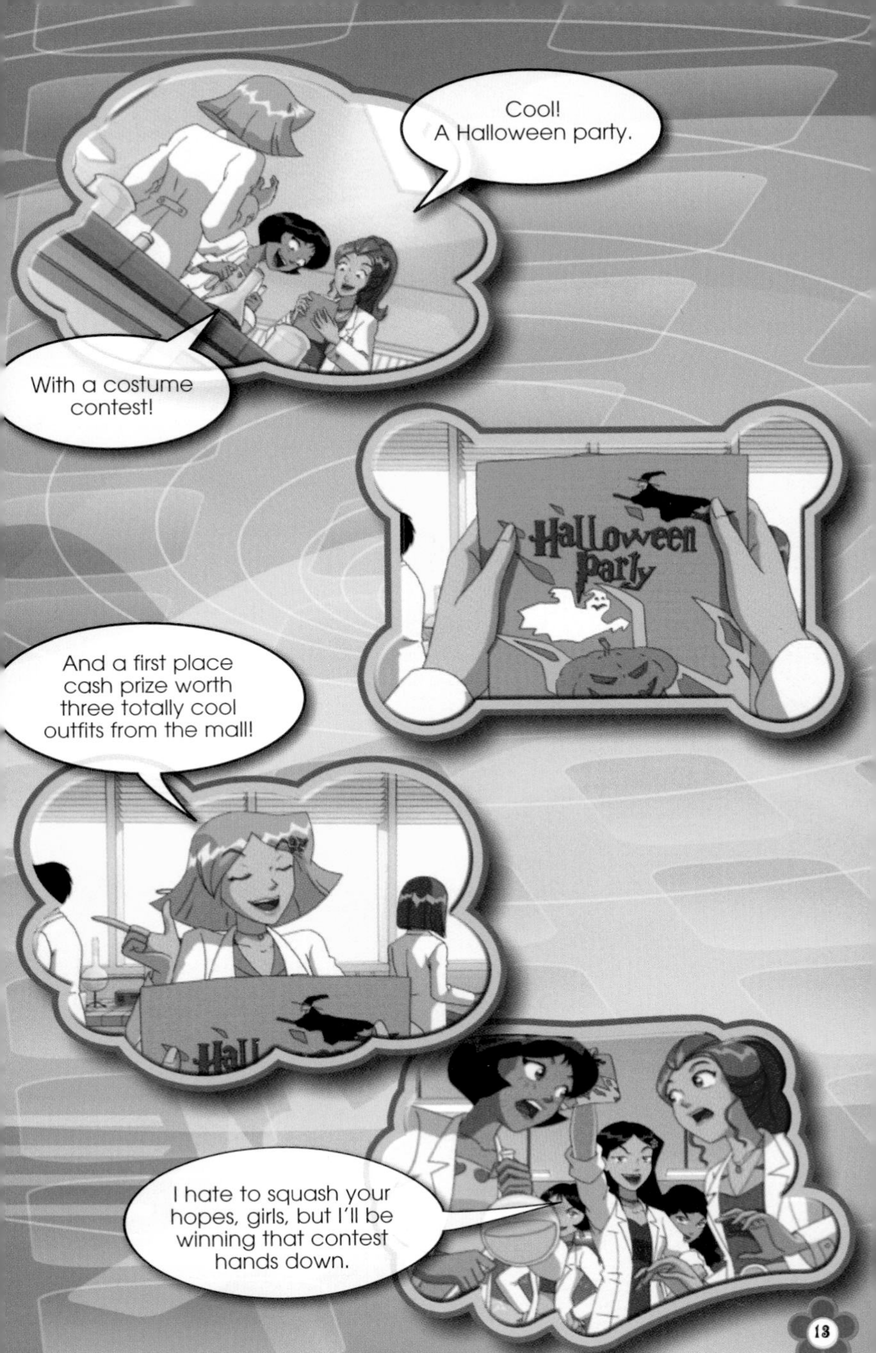
Cool! A Halloween party.
With a costume contest!
Halloween Party
And a first place cash prize worth three totally cool outfits from the mall!
I hate to squash your hopes, girls, but I'll be winning that contest hands down.

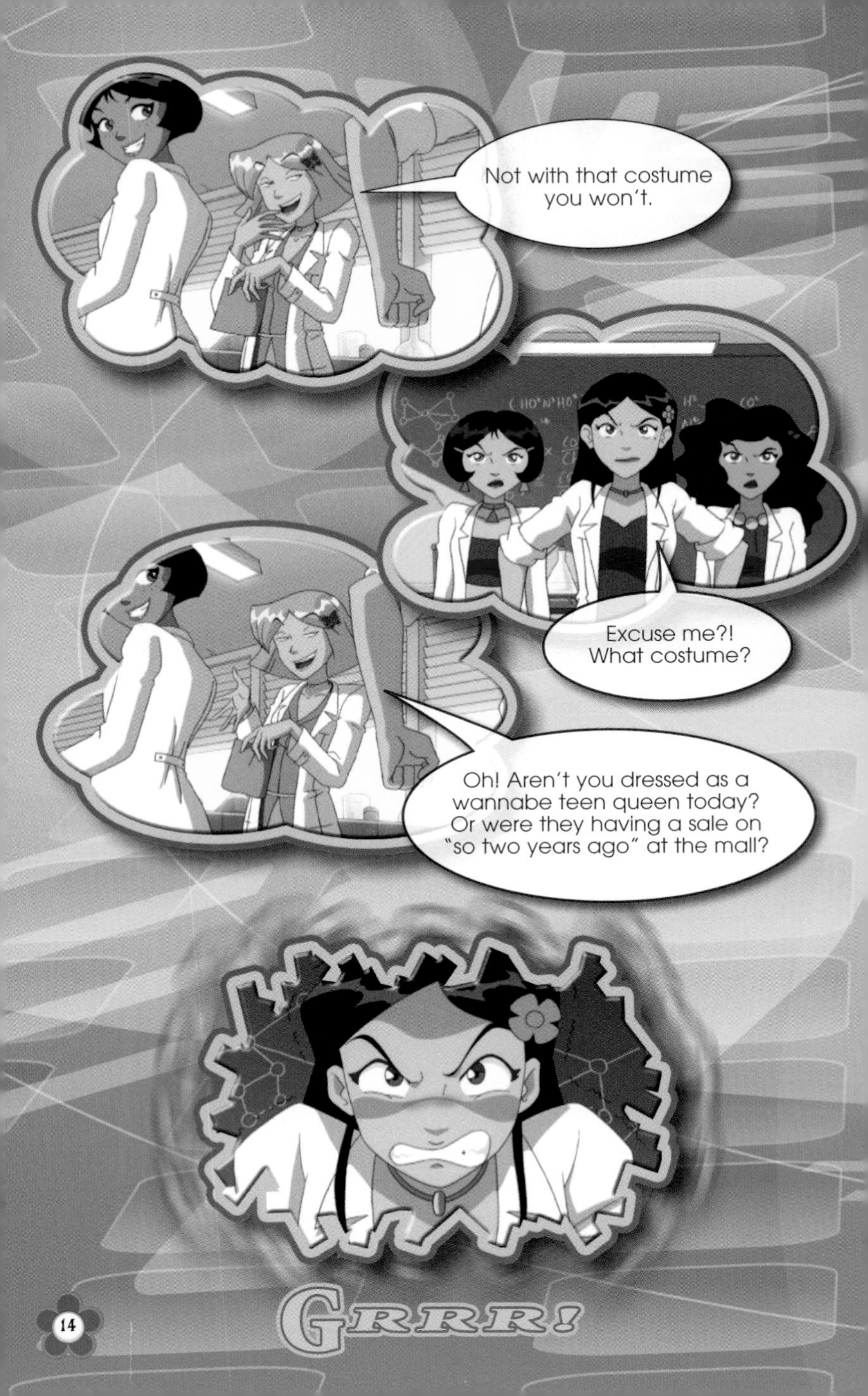
Not with that costume you won't.
Excuse me?! What costume?
Oh! Aren't you dressed as a wannabe teen queen today? Or were they having a sale on "so two years ago" at the mall?
GRRR!

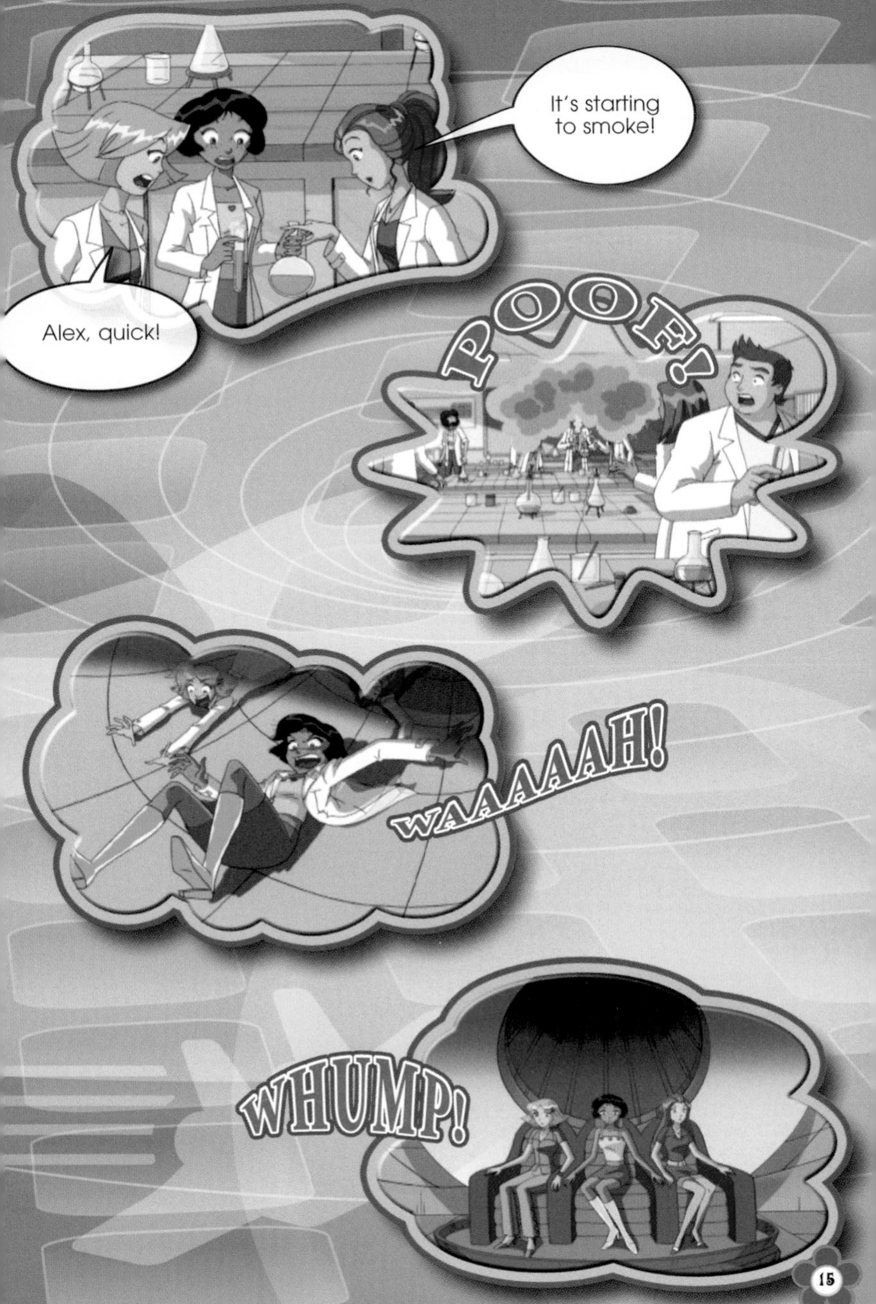

It's starting to smoke!
Alex, quick!
POOF!
WAAAAAH!
WHUMP!

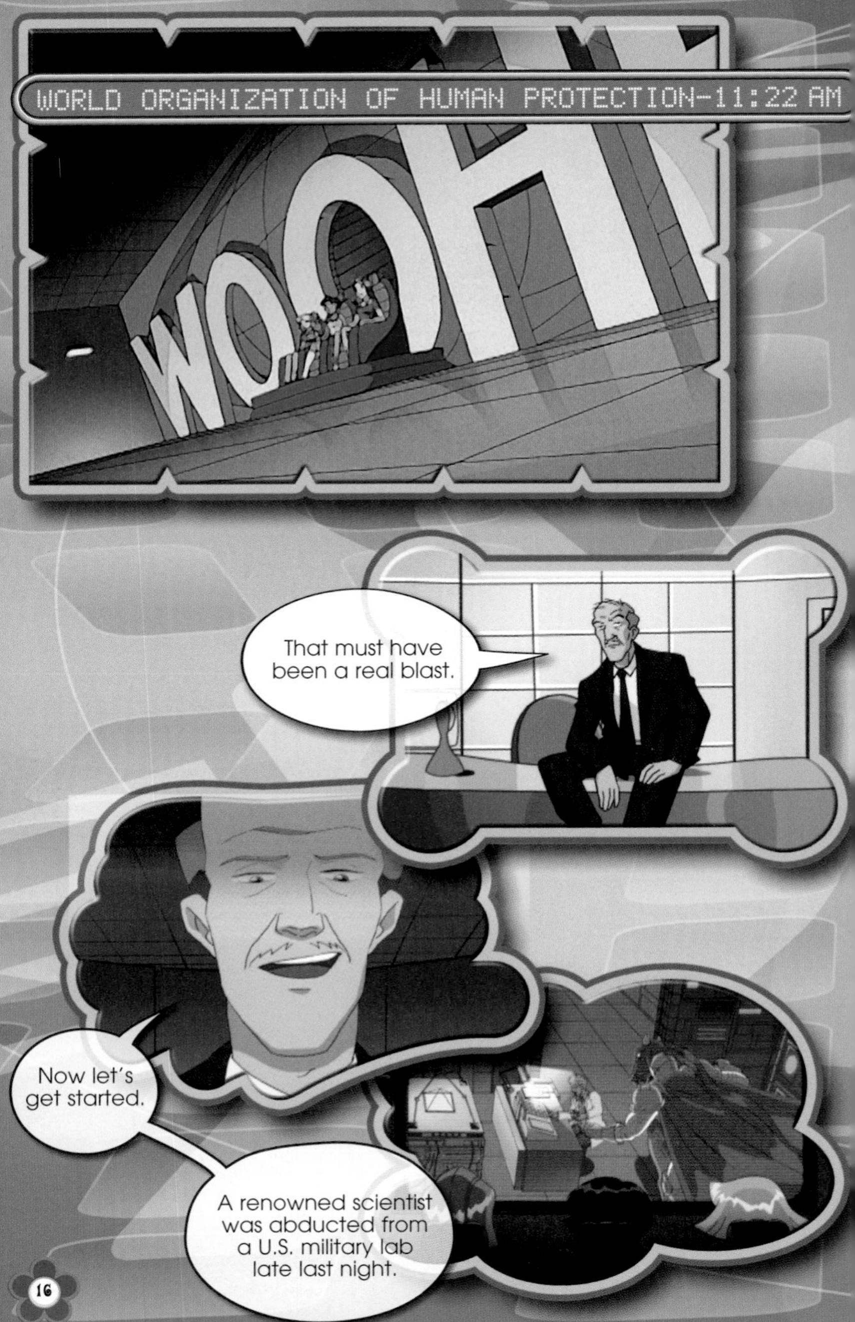
WORLD ORGANIZATION OF HUMAN PROTECTION-11:22 AM
WOOH
That must have been a real blast.
Now let's get started.
A renowned scientist was abducted from a U.S. military lab late last night.

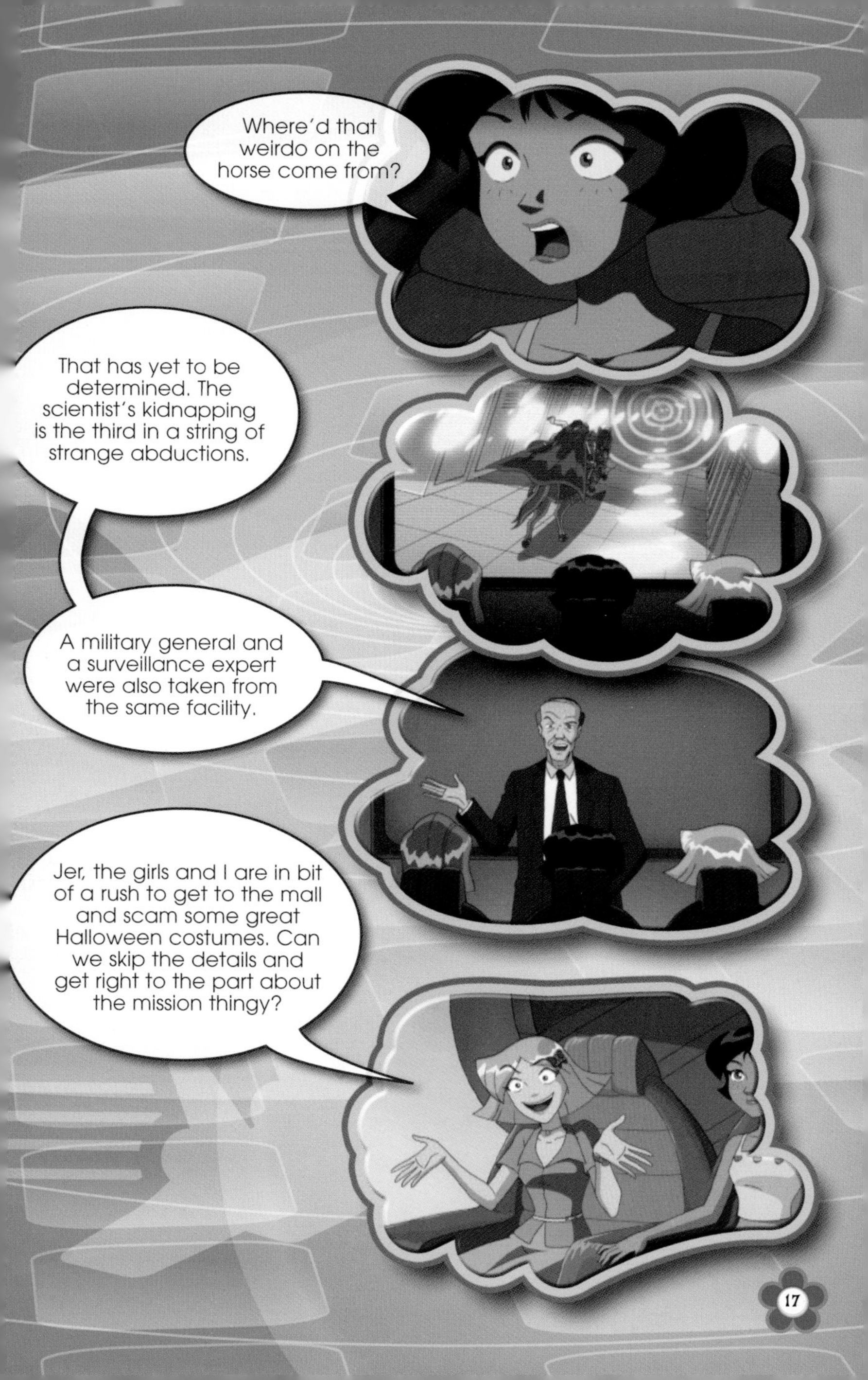
Where'd that weirdo on the horse come from?
That has yet to be determined. The scientist's kidnapping is the third in a string of strange abductions.
A military general and a surveillance expert were also taken from the same facility.
Jer, the girls and I are in bit of a rush to get to the mall and scam some great Halloween costumes. Can we skip the details and get right to the part about the mission thingy?

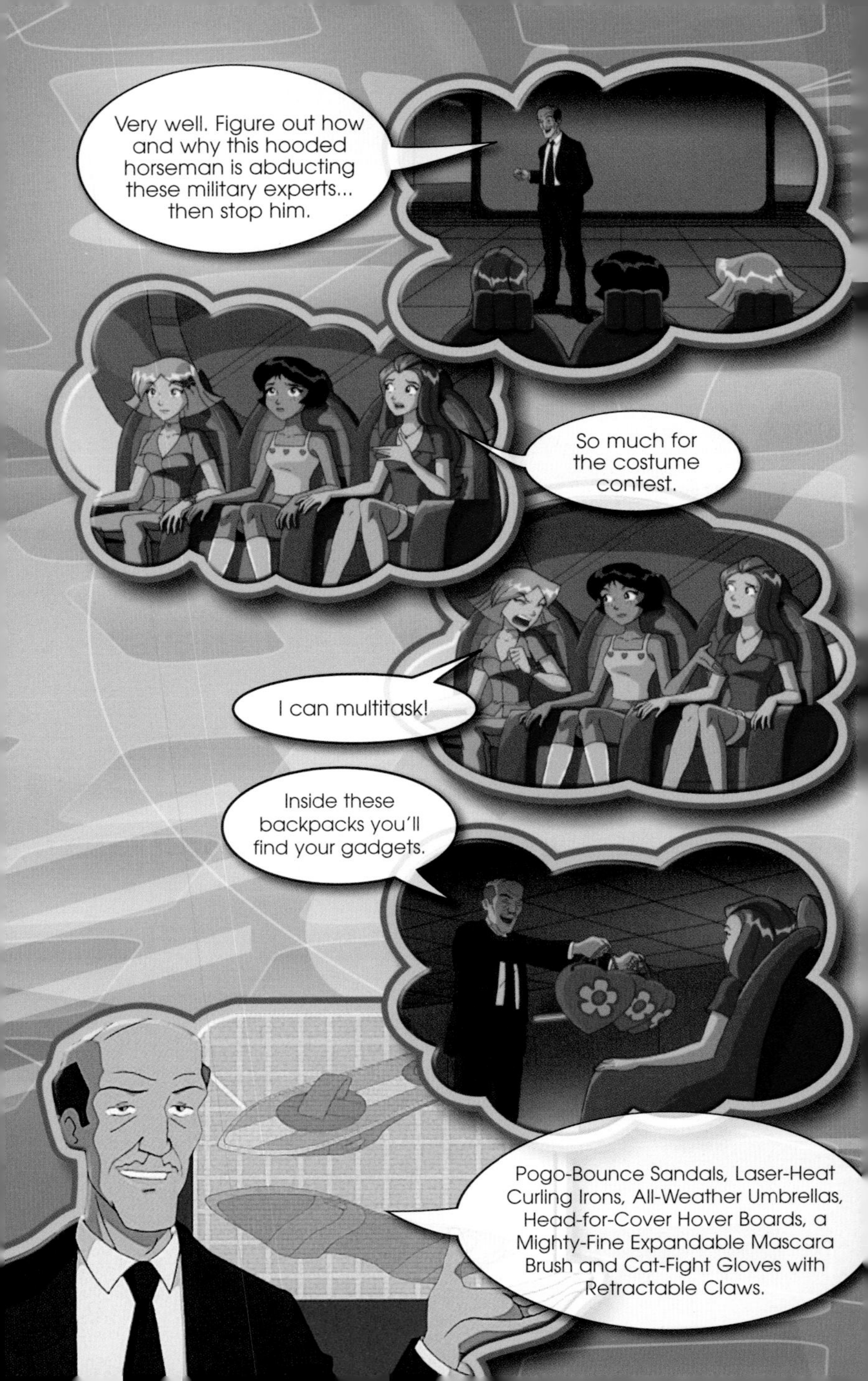
Very well. Figure out how and why this hooded horseman is abducting these military experts... then stop him.
So much for the costume contest.
I can multitask!
Inside these backpacks you'll find your gadgets.
Pogo-Bounce Sandals, Laser-Heat Curling Irons, All-Weather Umbrellas, Head-for-Cover Hover Boards, a Mighty-Fine Expandable Mascara Brush and Cat-Fight Gloves with Retractable Claws.

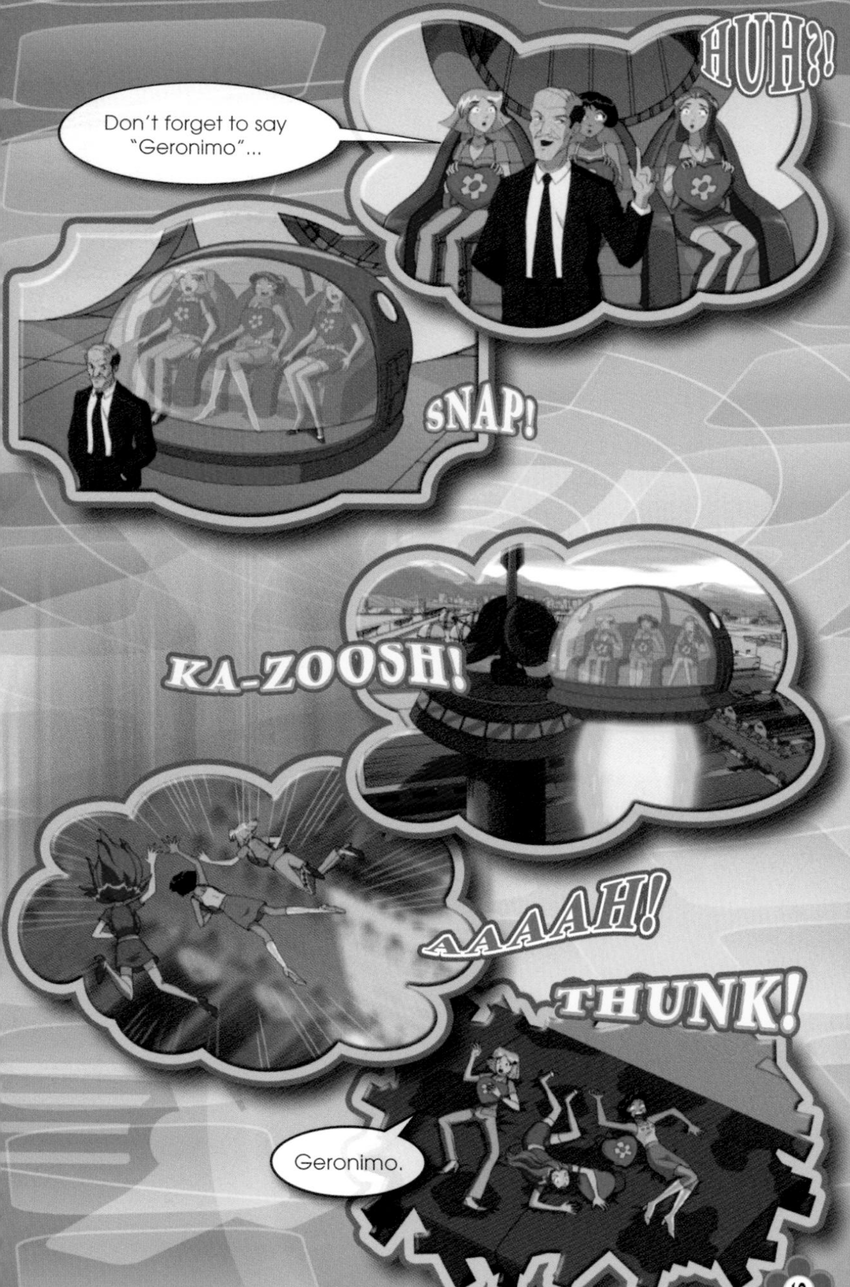
HUH?!
Don't forget to say "Geronimo"...
SNAP!
KA-ZOOSH!
AAAAH!
THUNK!
Geronimo.

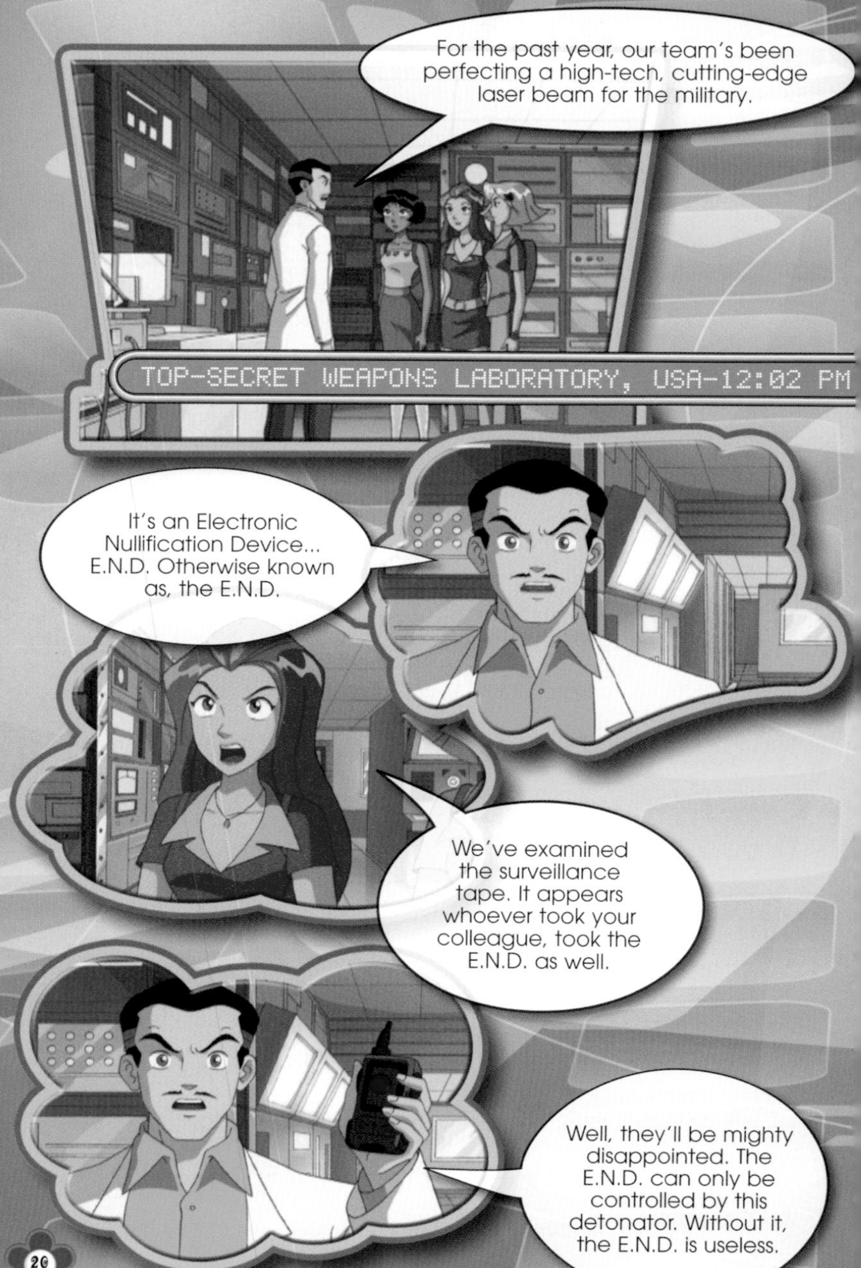
For the past year, our team's been perfecting a high-tech, cutting-edge laser beam for the military.
TOP-SECRET WEAPONS LABORATORY, USA-12:02 PM
It's an Electronic Nullification Device... E.N.D. Otherwise known as, the E.N.D.
We've examined the surveillance tape. It appears whoever took your colleague, took the E.N.D. as well.
Well, they'll be mighty disappointed. The E.N.D. can only be controlled by this detonator. Without it, the E.N.D. is useless.

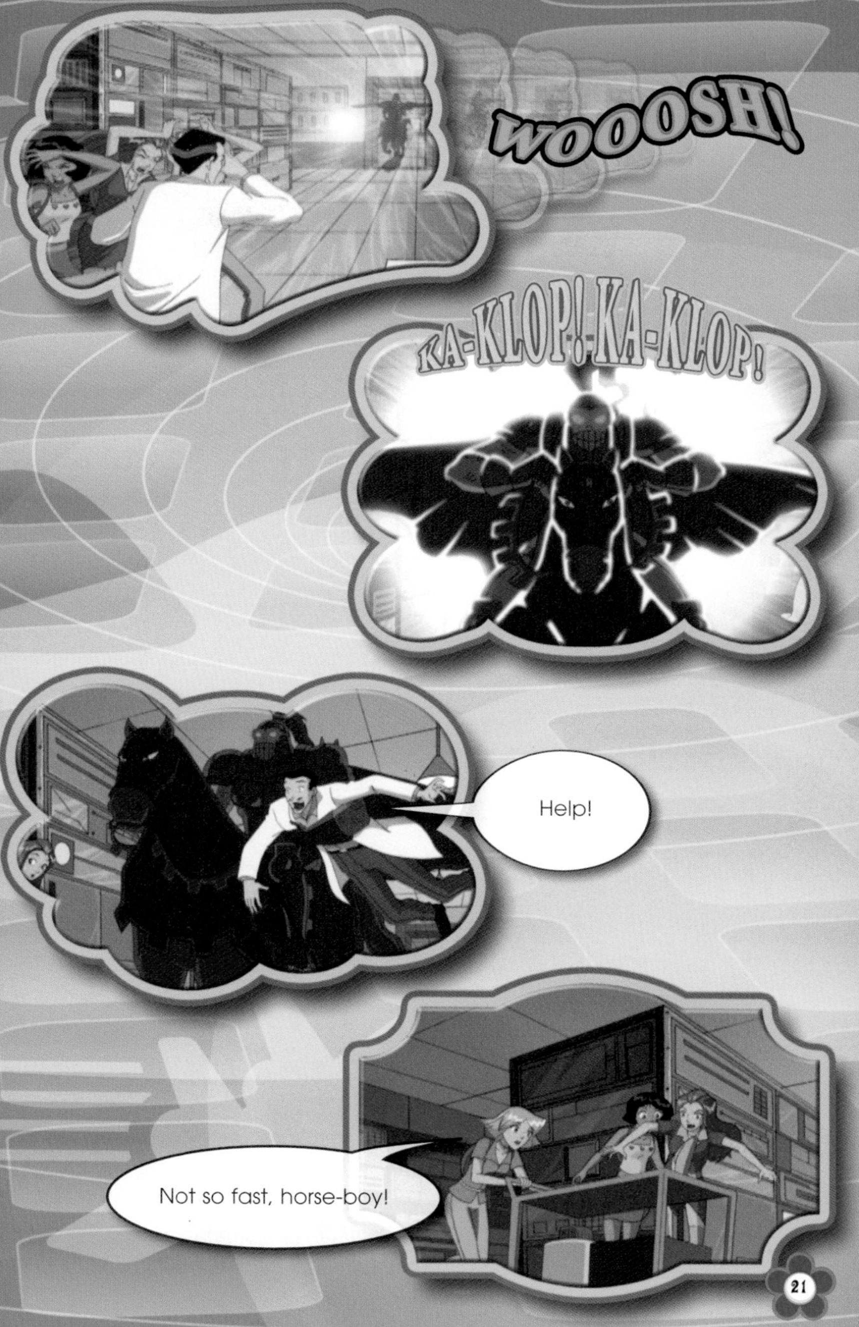
WOOOOSH!
KA-KLOP! KA-KLOP!
Help!
Not so fast, horse-boy!

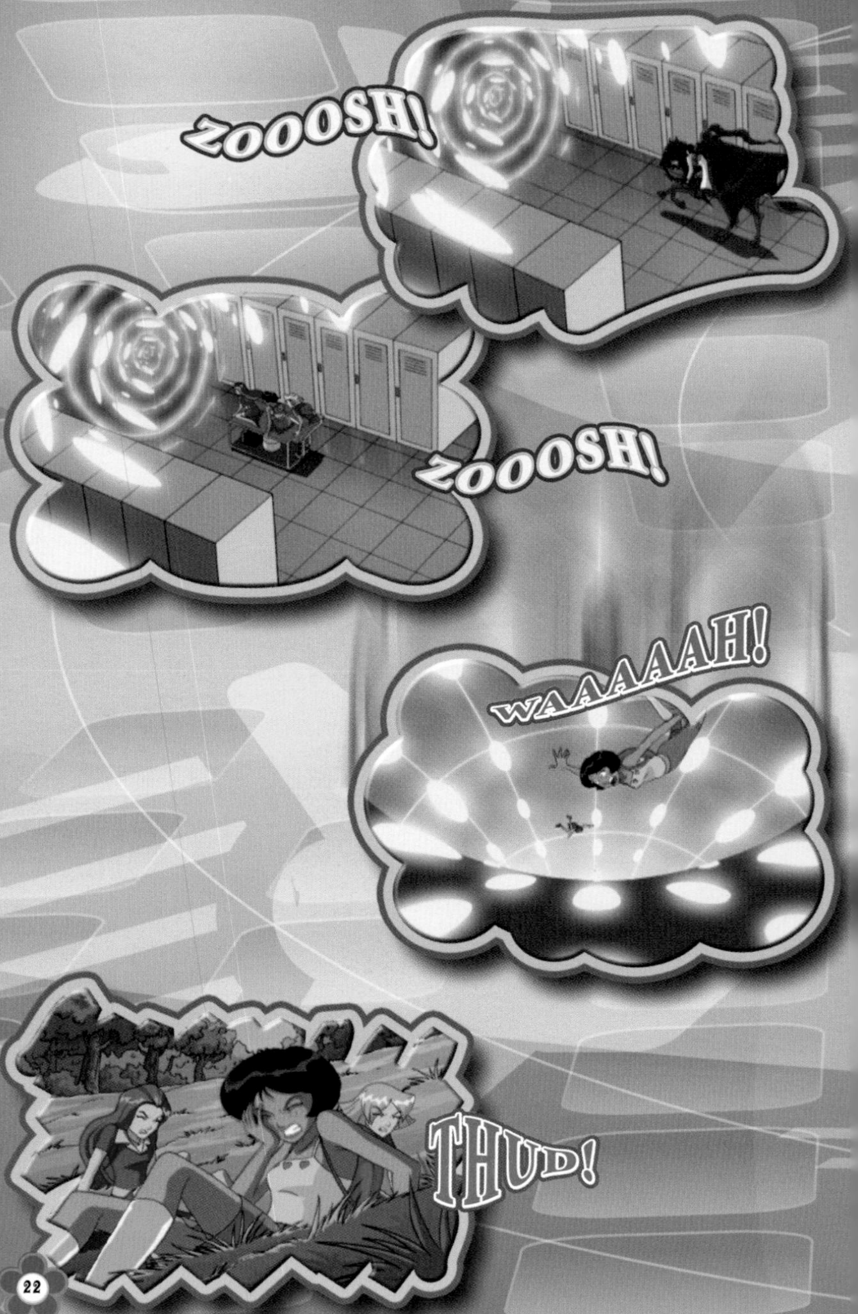
ZOOOSH!
ZOOOSH!
WAAAAAH!
THUD!

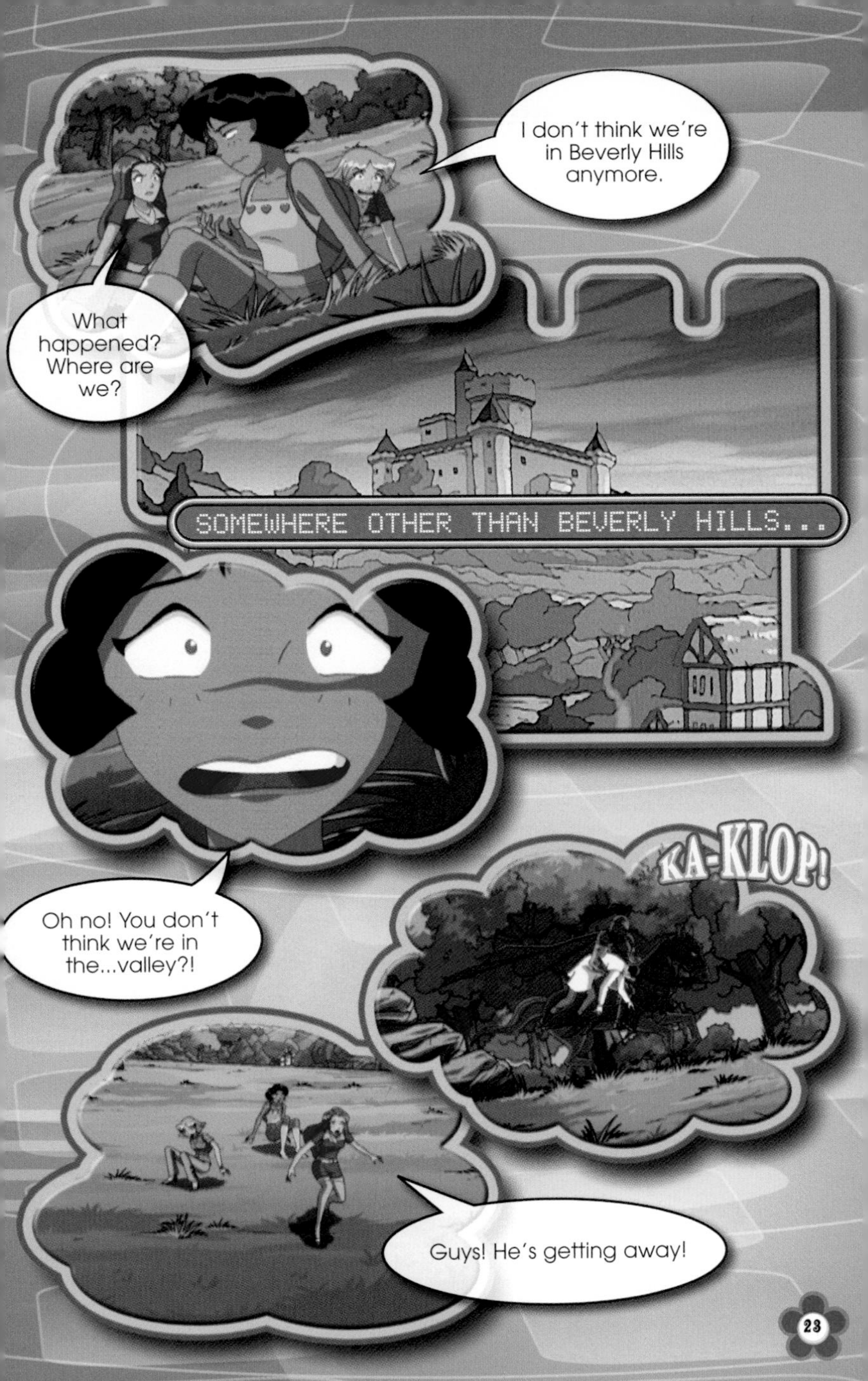
I don't think we're in Beverly Hills anymore.
What happened? Where are we?
SOMEWHERE OTHER THAN BEVERLY HILLS...
Oh no! You don't think we're in the...valley?!
KA-KLOP!
Guys! He's getting away!

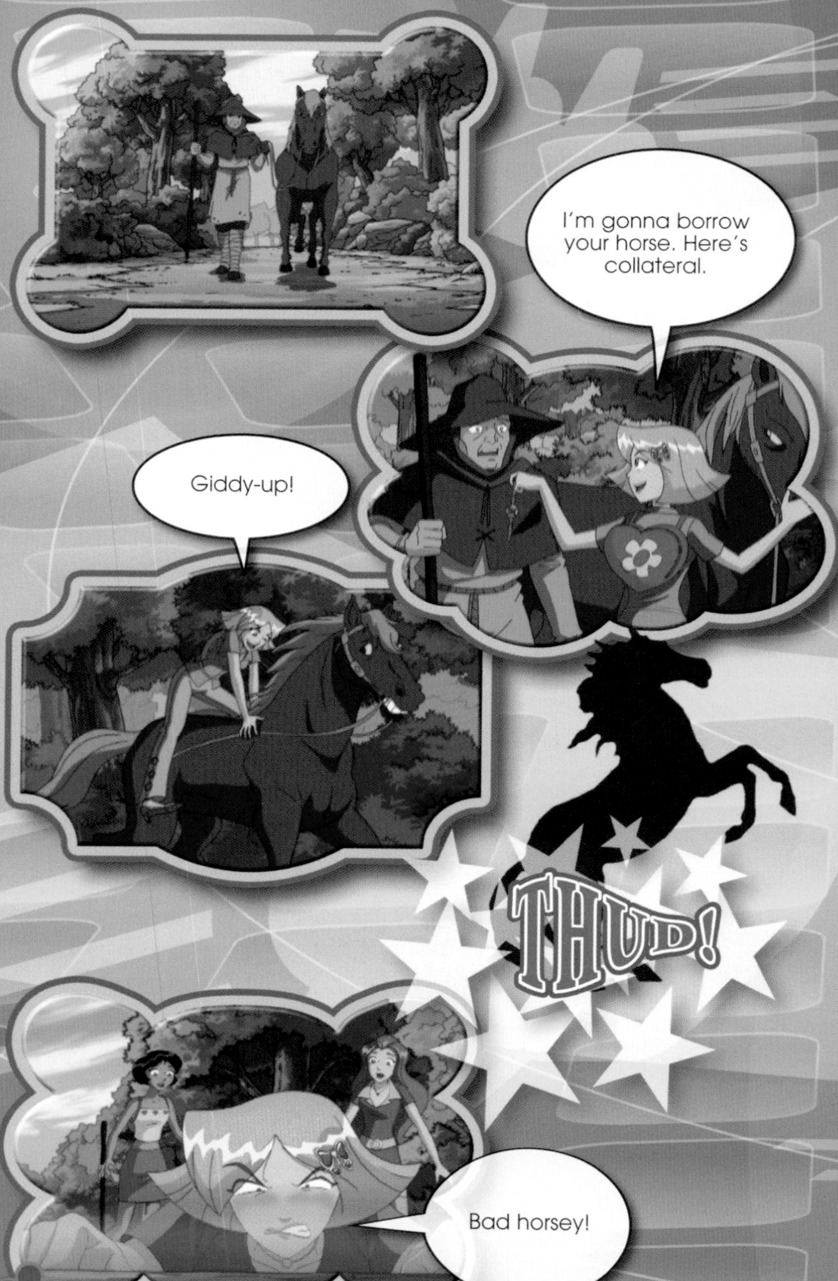
I'm gonna borrow your horse. Here's collateral.
Giddy-up!
THUD!
Bad horsey!

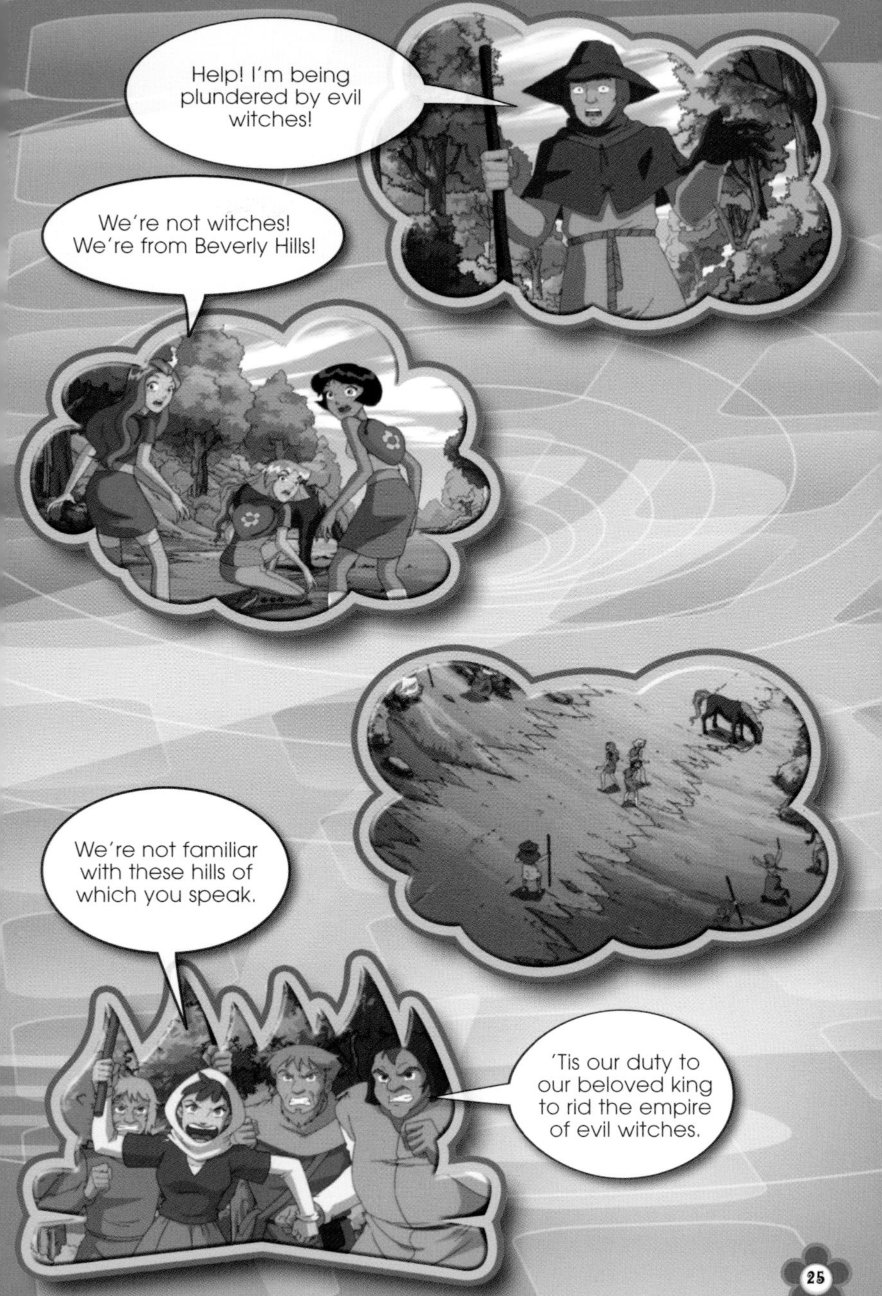
Help! I'm being plundered by evil witches!
We're not witches! We're from Beverly Hills!
We're not familiar with these hills of which you speak.
'Tis our duty to our beloved king to rid the empire of evil witches.

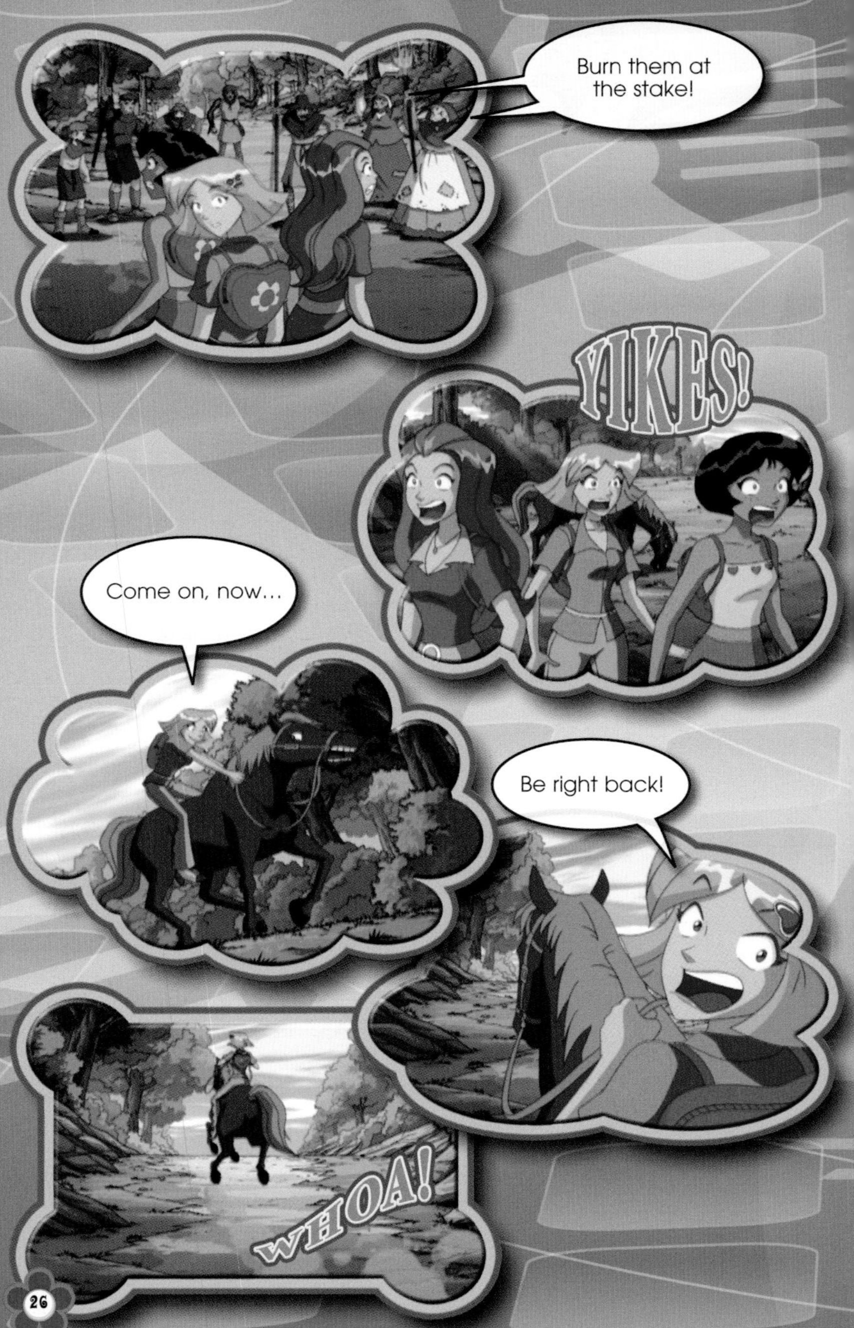

Burn them at the stake!
YIKES!
Come on, now...
Be right back!
WHOA!

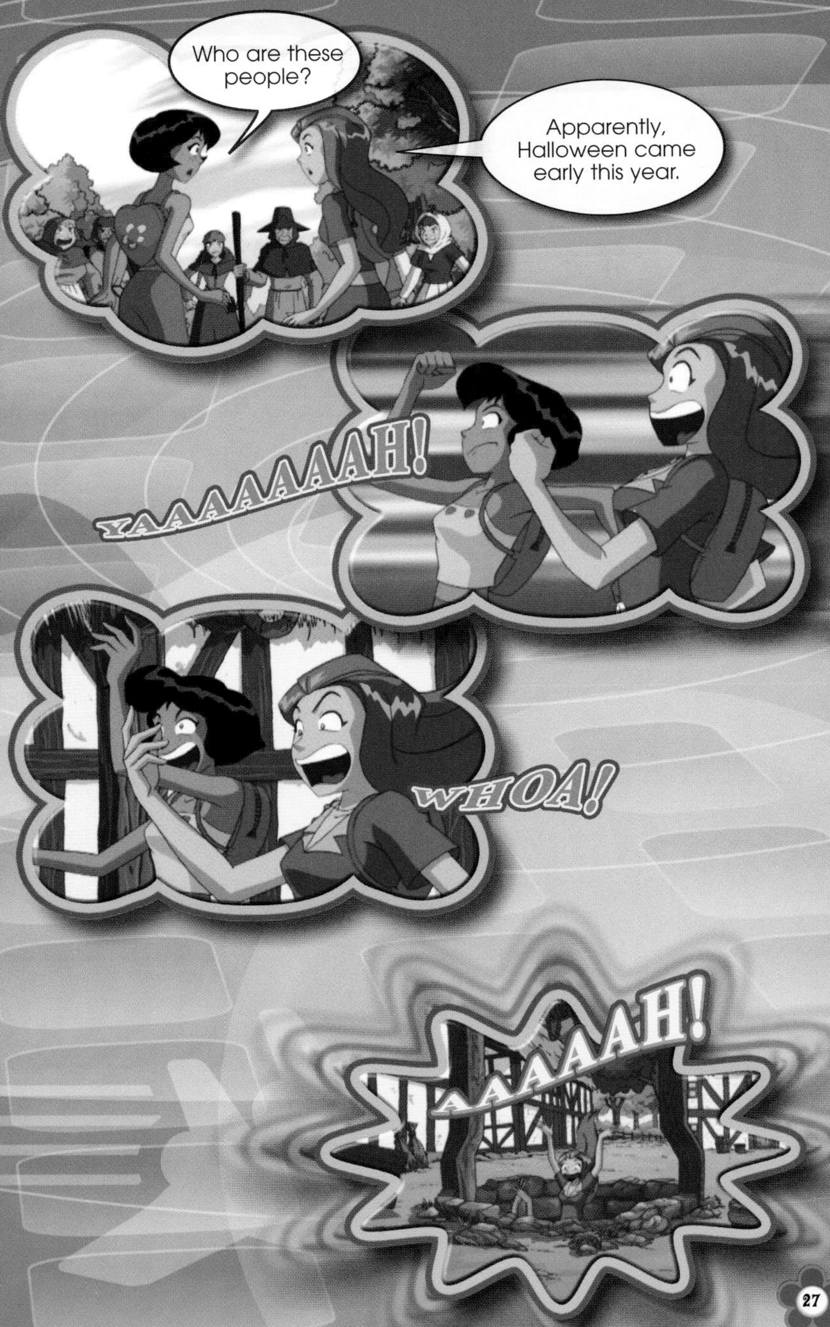

Who are these people?
Apparently, Halloween came early this year.
YAAAAAAAAH!
WHOA!
AAAAAAH!

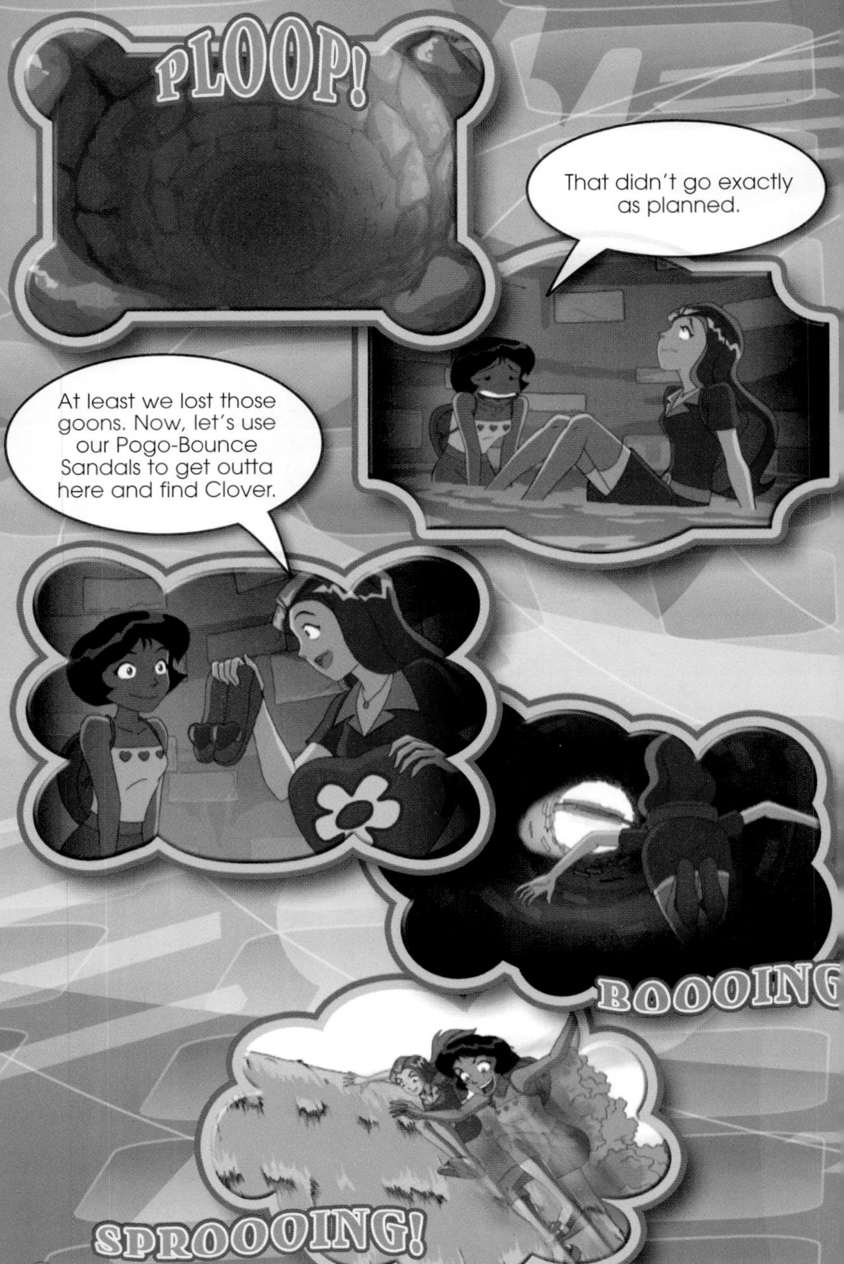
PLOOP!
That didn't go exactly as planned.
At least we lost those goons. Now, let's use our Pogo-Bounce Sandals to get outta here and find Clover.
BOOOING
SPROOOOING!

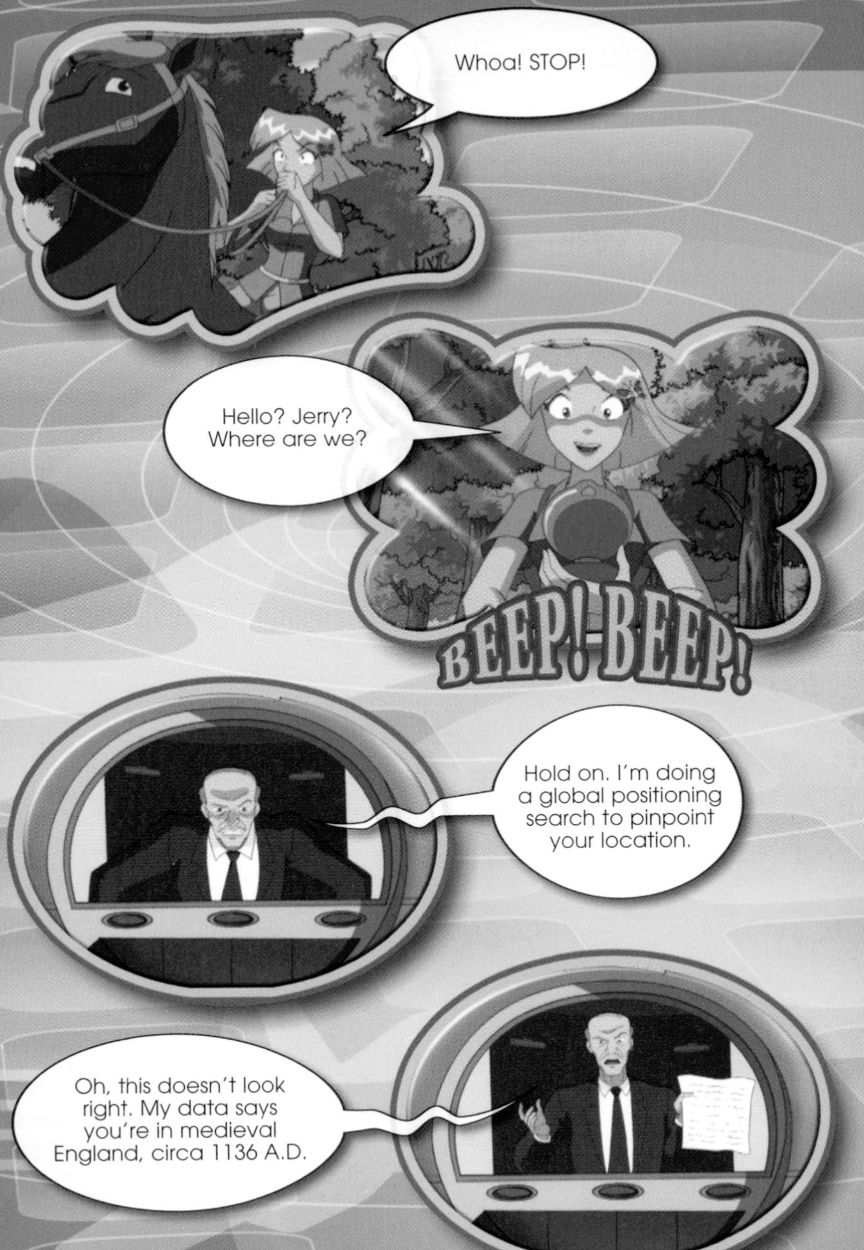
Whoa! STOP!
Hello? Jerry? Where are we?
BEEP! BEEP!
Hold on. I'm doing a global positioning search to pinpoint your location.
Oh, this doesn't look right. My data says you're in medieval England, circa 1136 A.D.

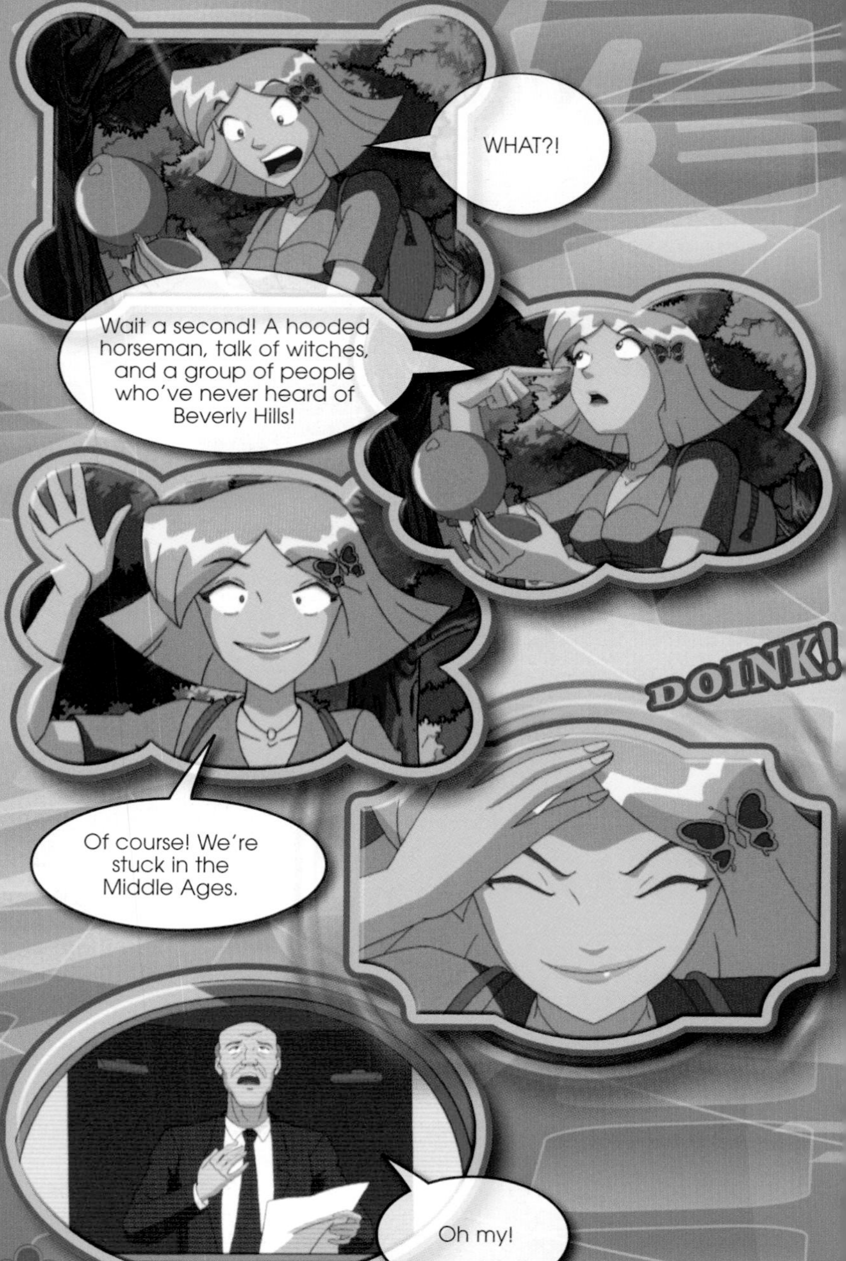
WHAT?!
Wait a second! A hooded horseman, talk of witches, and a group of people who've never heard of Beverly Hills!
Of course! We're stuck in the Middle Ages.
DOINK!
Oh my!

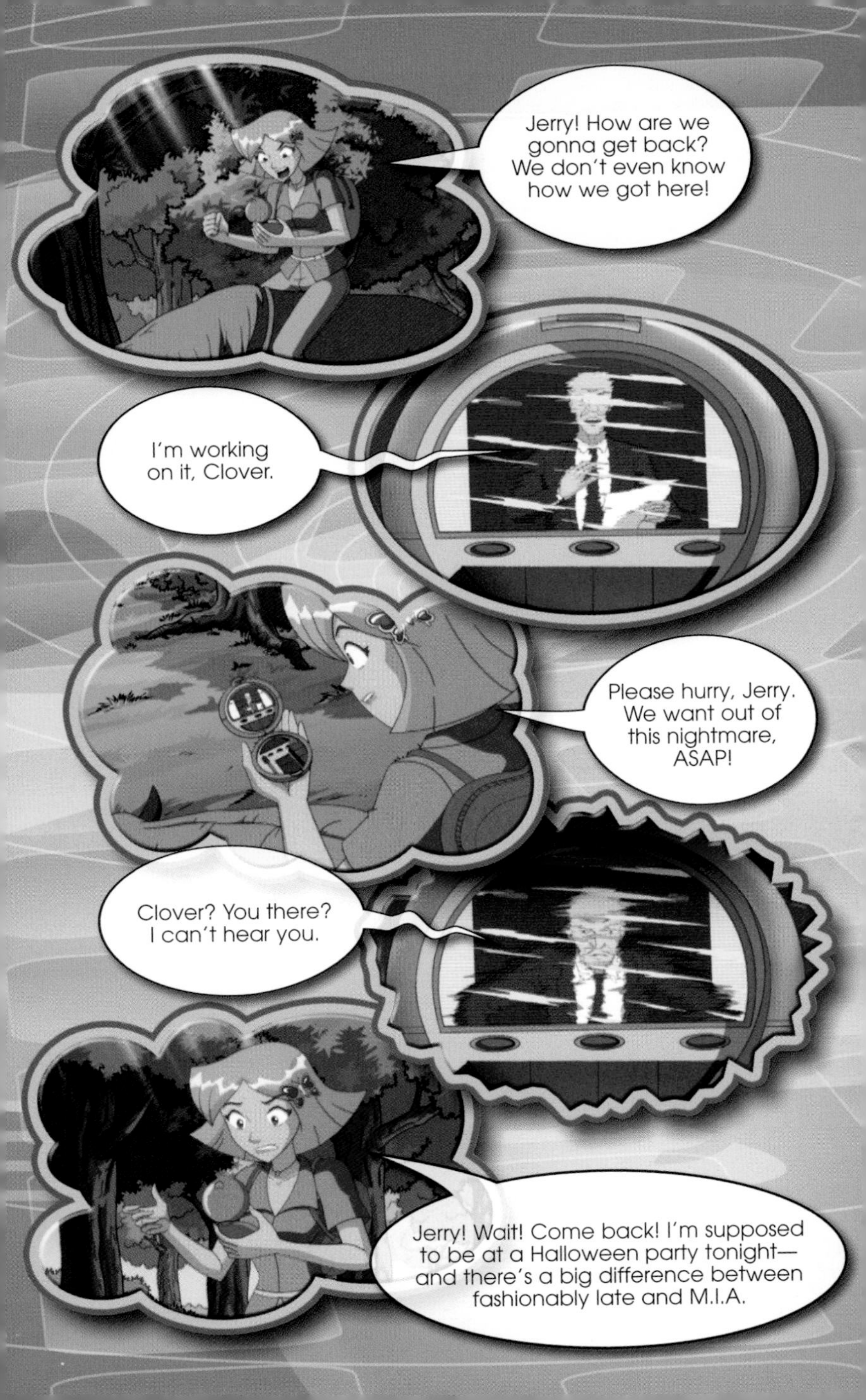
Jerry! How are we gonna get back? We don't even know how we got here!
I'm working on it, Clover.
Please hurry, Jerry. We want out of this nightmare, ASAP!
Clover? You there? I can't hear you.
Jerry! Wait! Come back! I'm supposed to be at a Halloween party tonight—and there's a big difference between fashionably late and M.I.A.

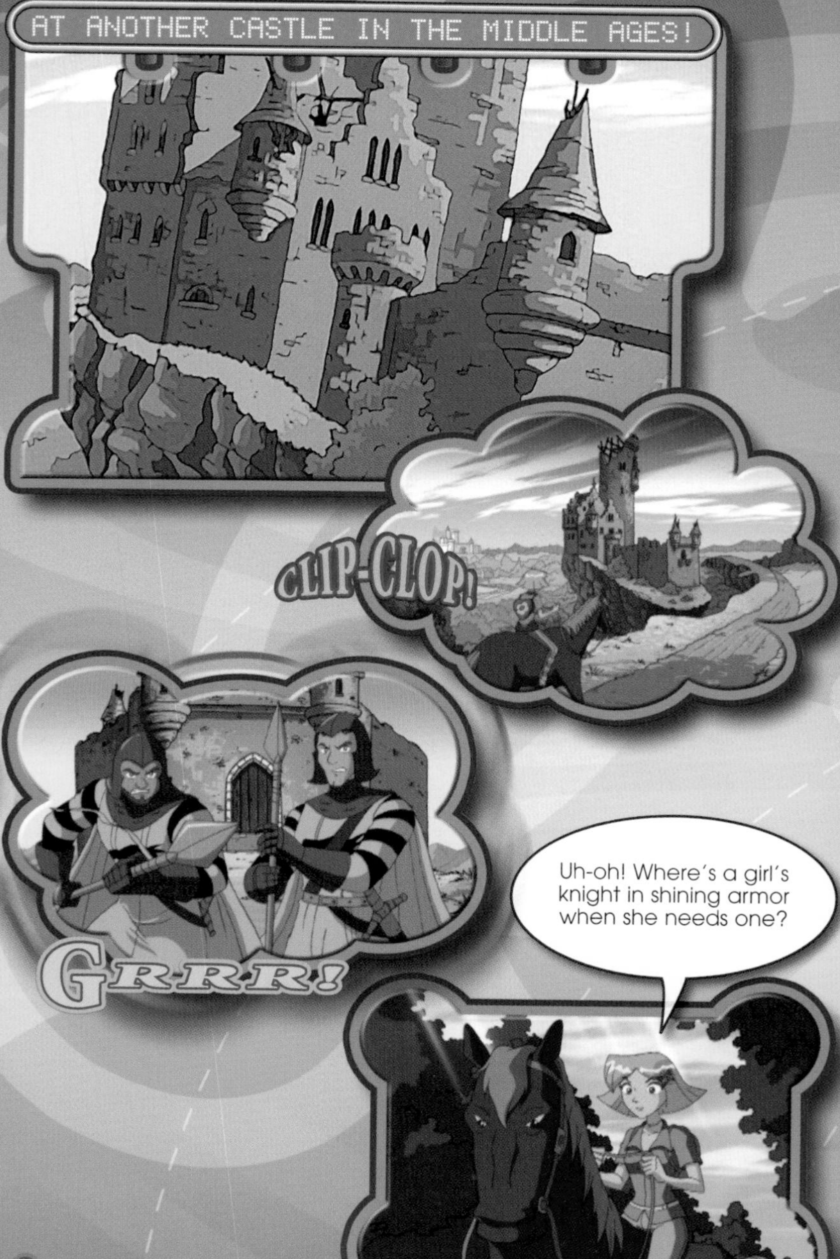
AT ANOTHER CASTLE IN THE MIDDLE AGES!
CLIP-CLOP!
GRRRR!
Uh-oh! Where's a girl's knight in shining armor when she needs one?

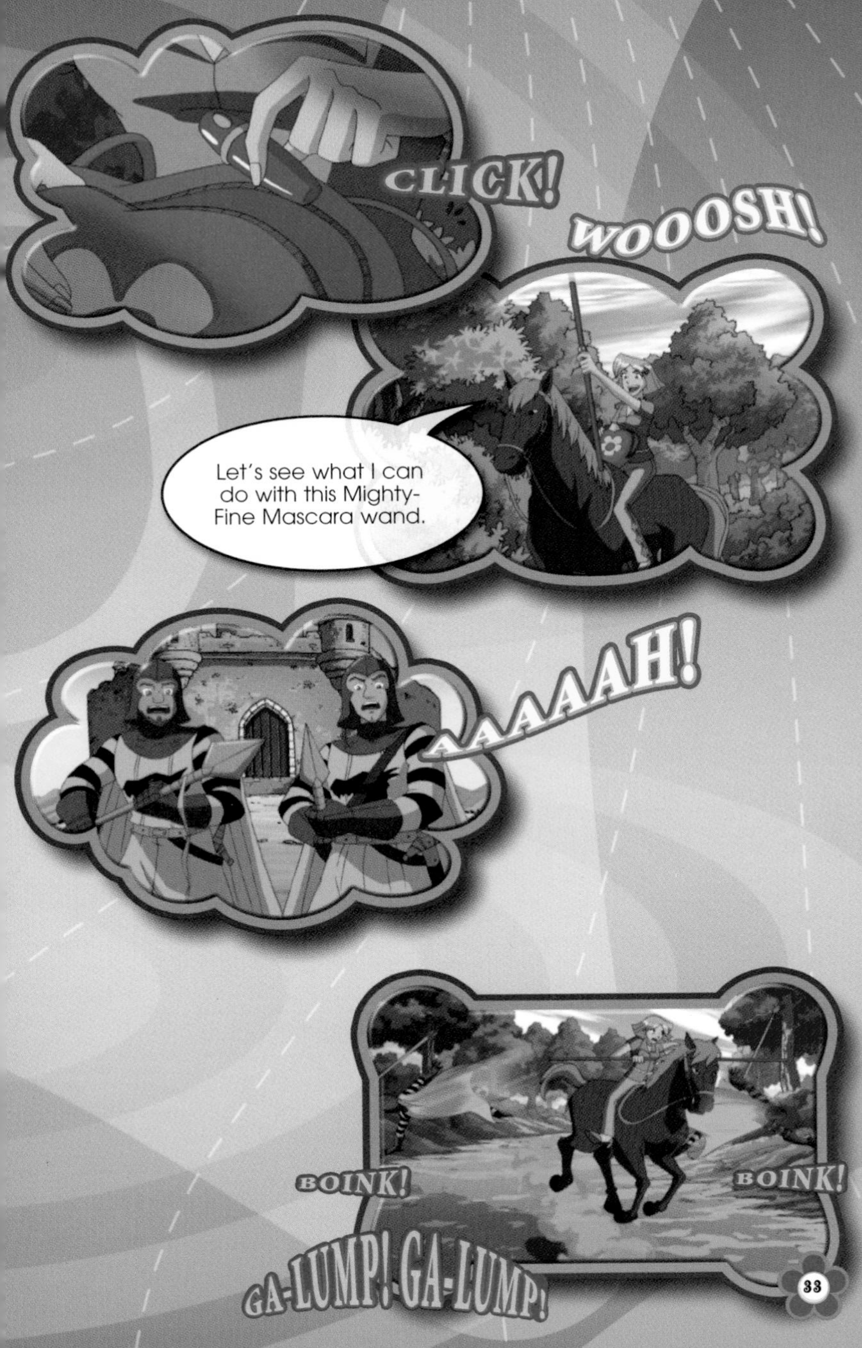
CLICK!
WOOOSH!
Let's see what I can do with this Mighty-Fine Mascara wand.
AAAAAAH!
BOINK!
BOINK!
GA-LUMP! GA-LUMP!

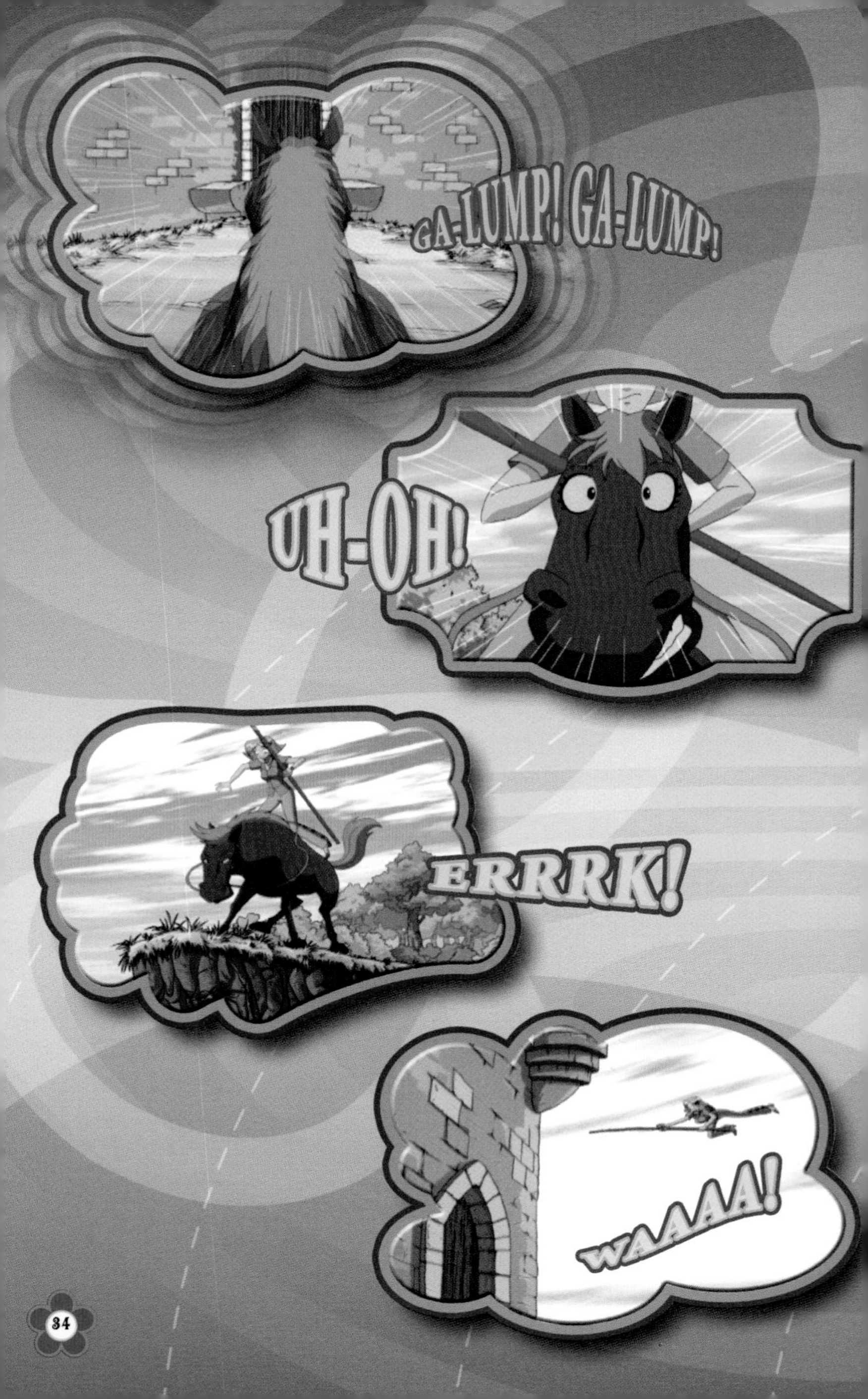
GA-LUMP! GA-LUMP!
UH-OH!
ERRRK!
WAAAA!

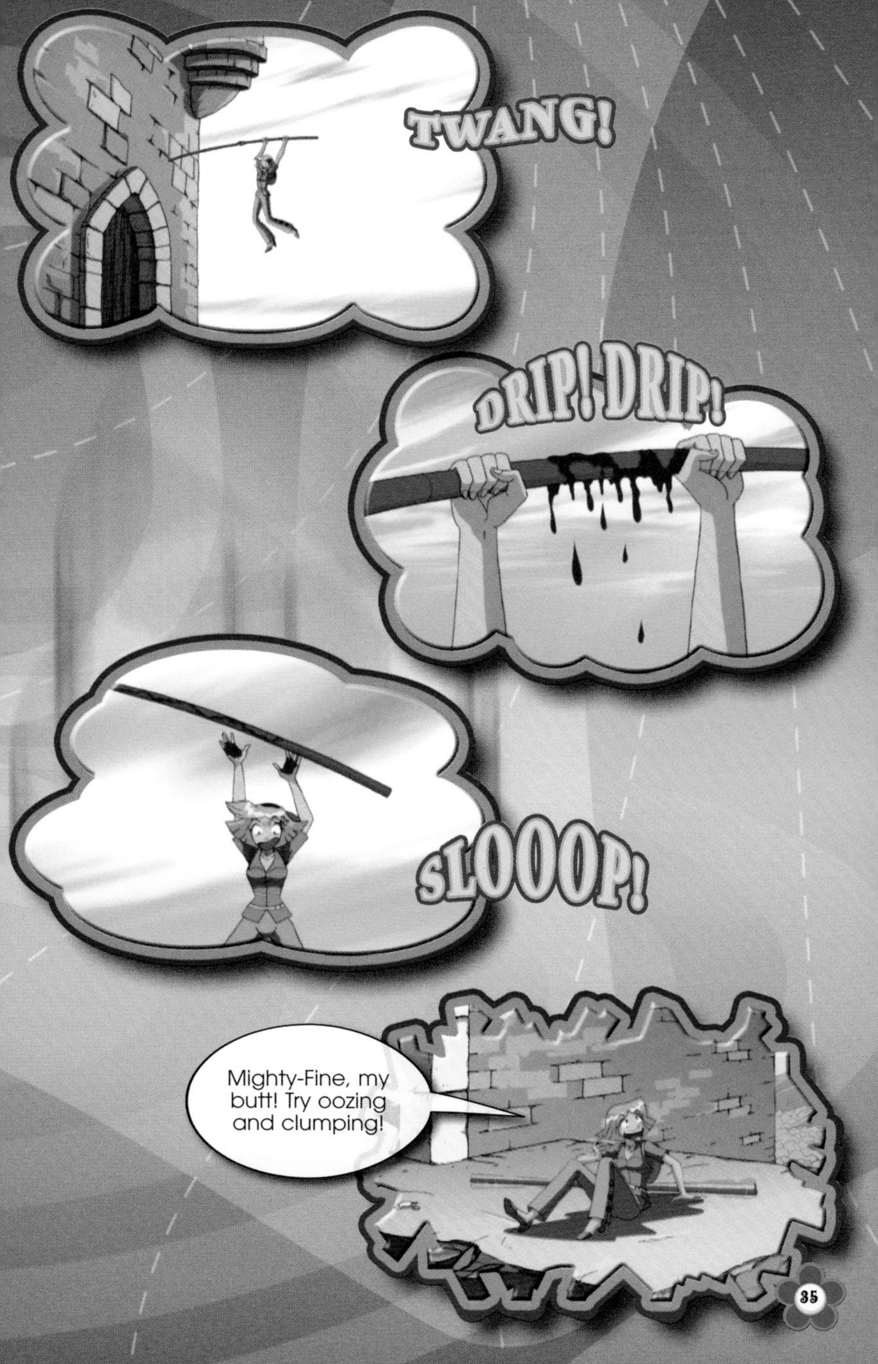
TWANG!
DRIP! DRIP!
SLOOOP!
Mighty-Fine, my butt! Try oozing and clumping!

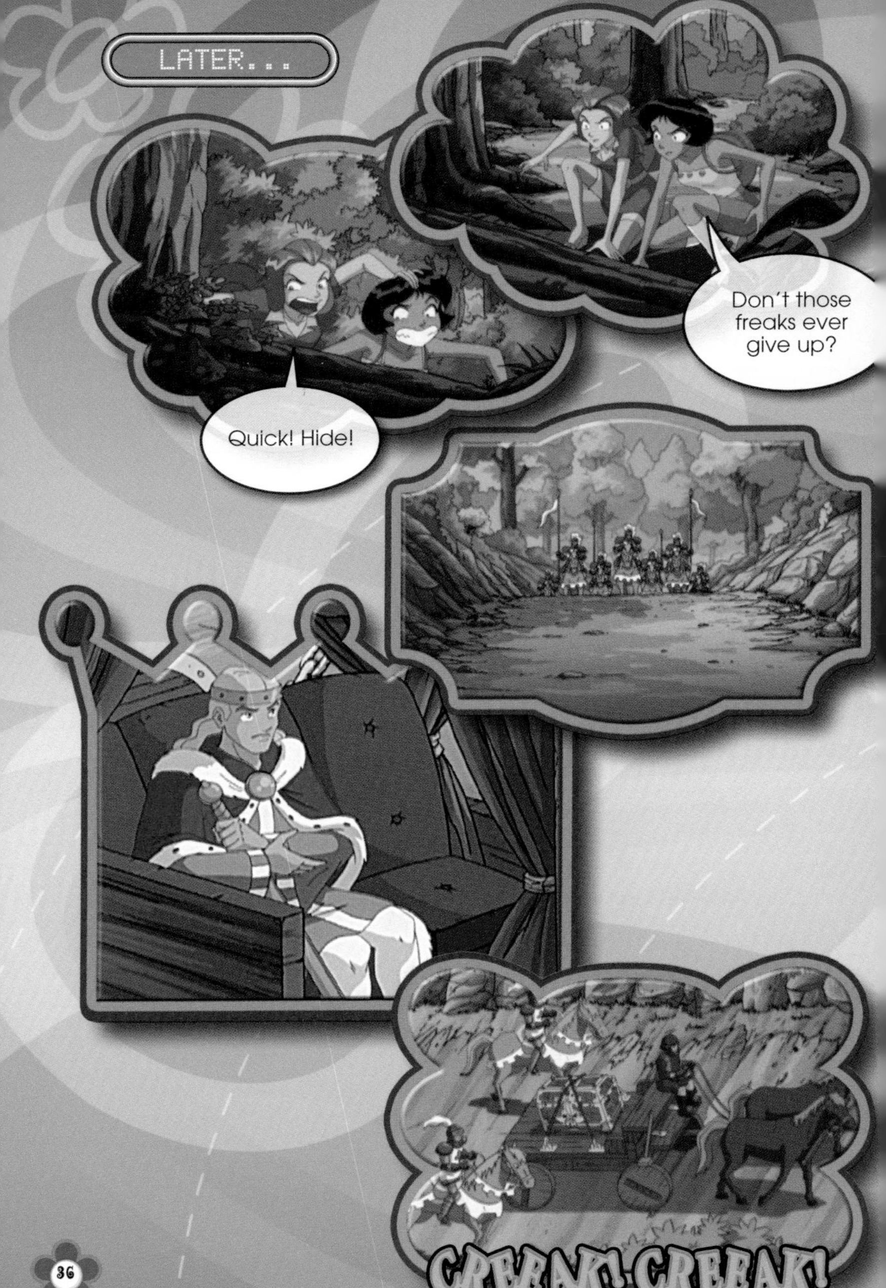
LATER...
Quick! Hide!
Don't those freaks ever give up?
CREEAK! CREEAK!

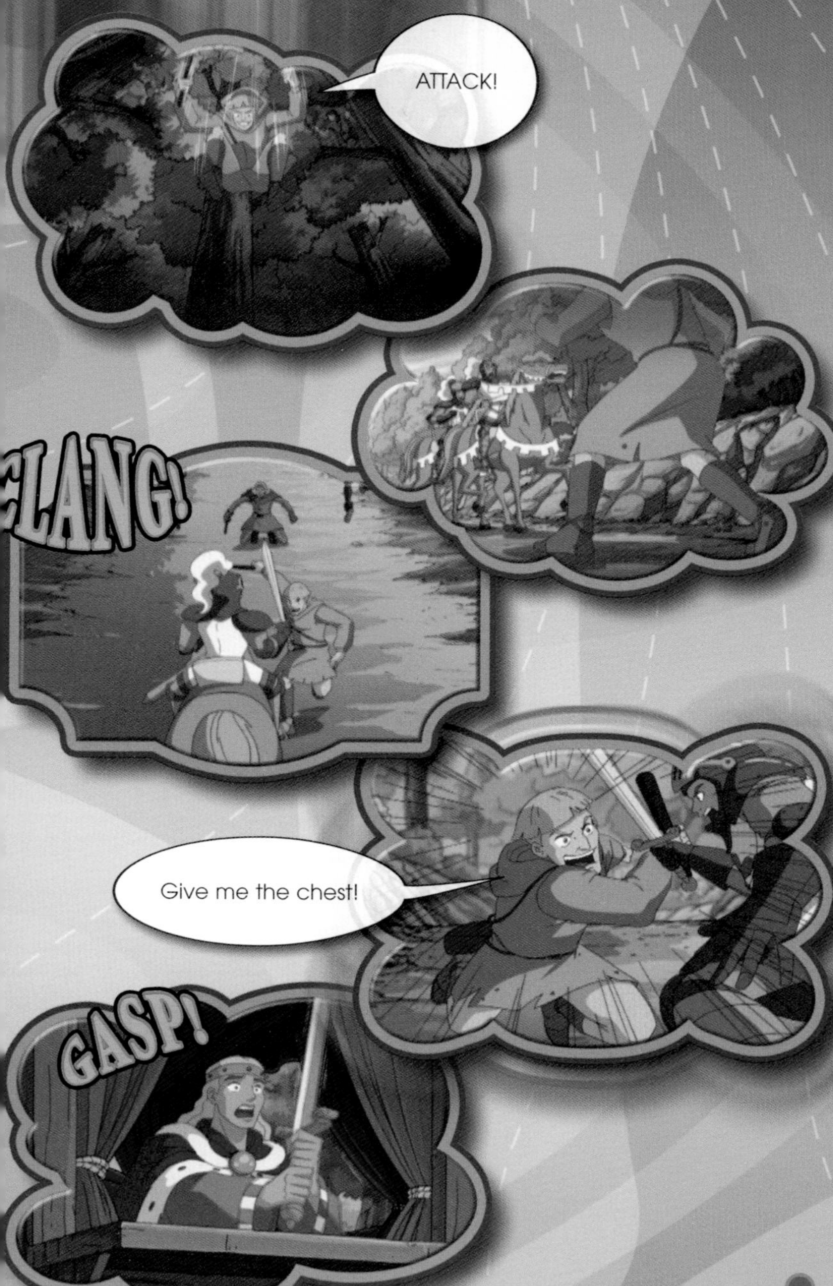
ATTACK!
CLANG!
Give me the chest!
GASP!

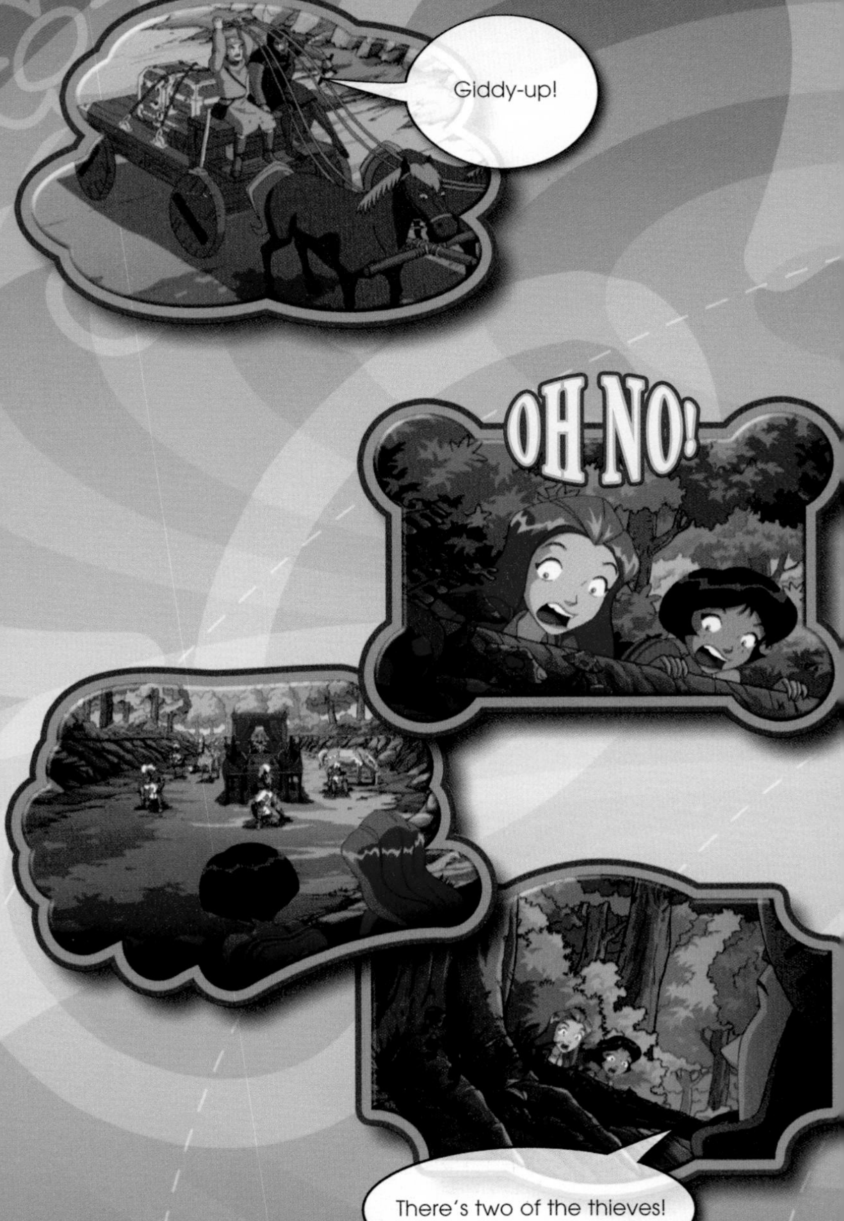
Giddy-up!
OH NO!
There's two of the thieves!

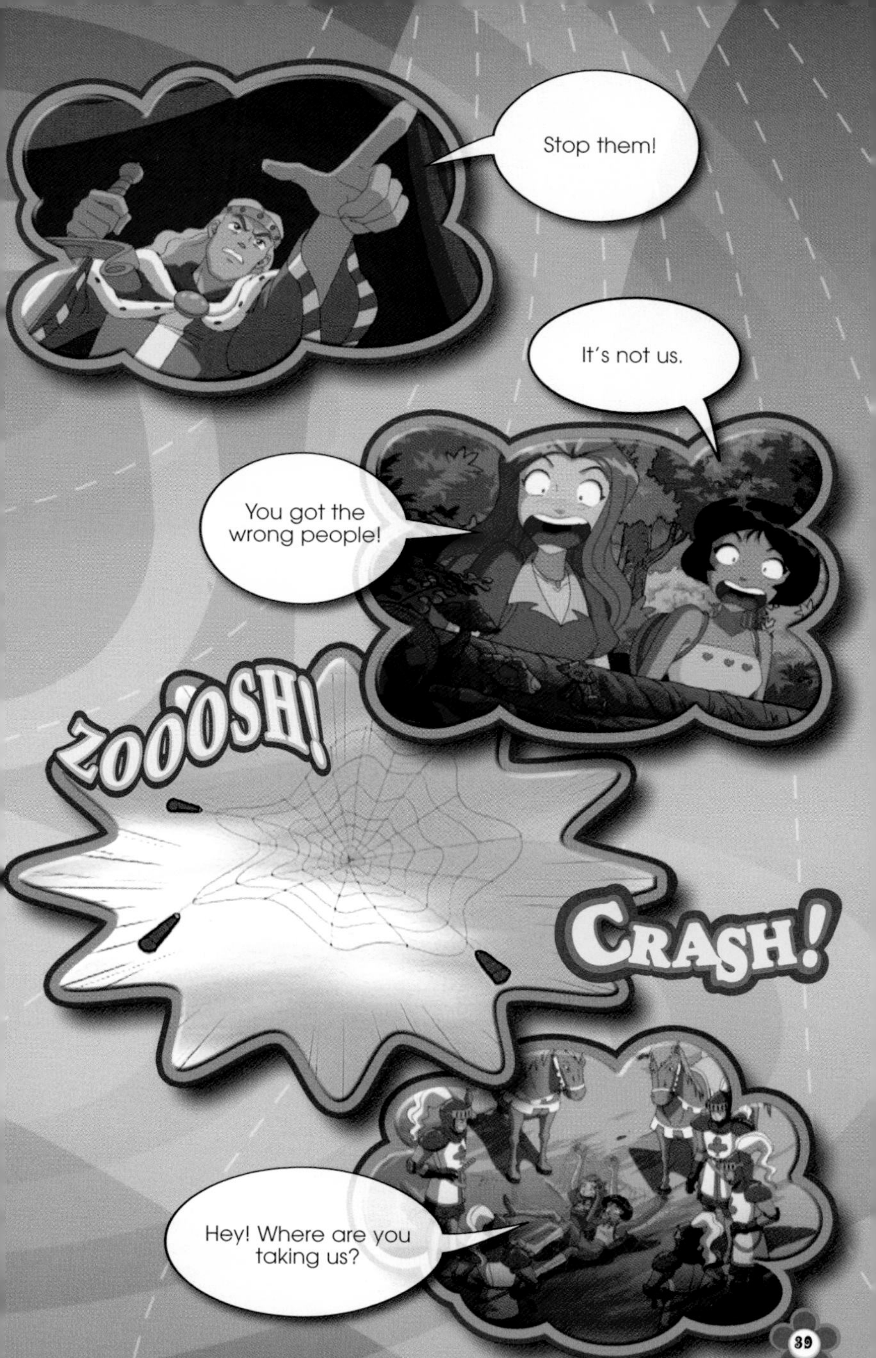
Stop them!
It's not us.
You got the wrong people!
ZOOOSH!
CRASH!
Hey! Where are you taking us?

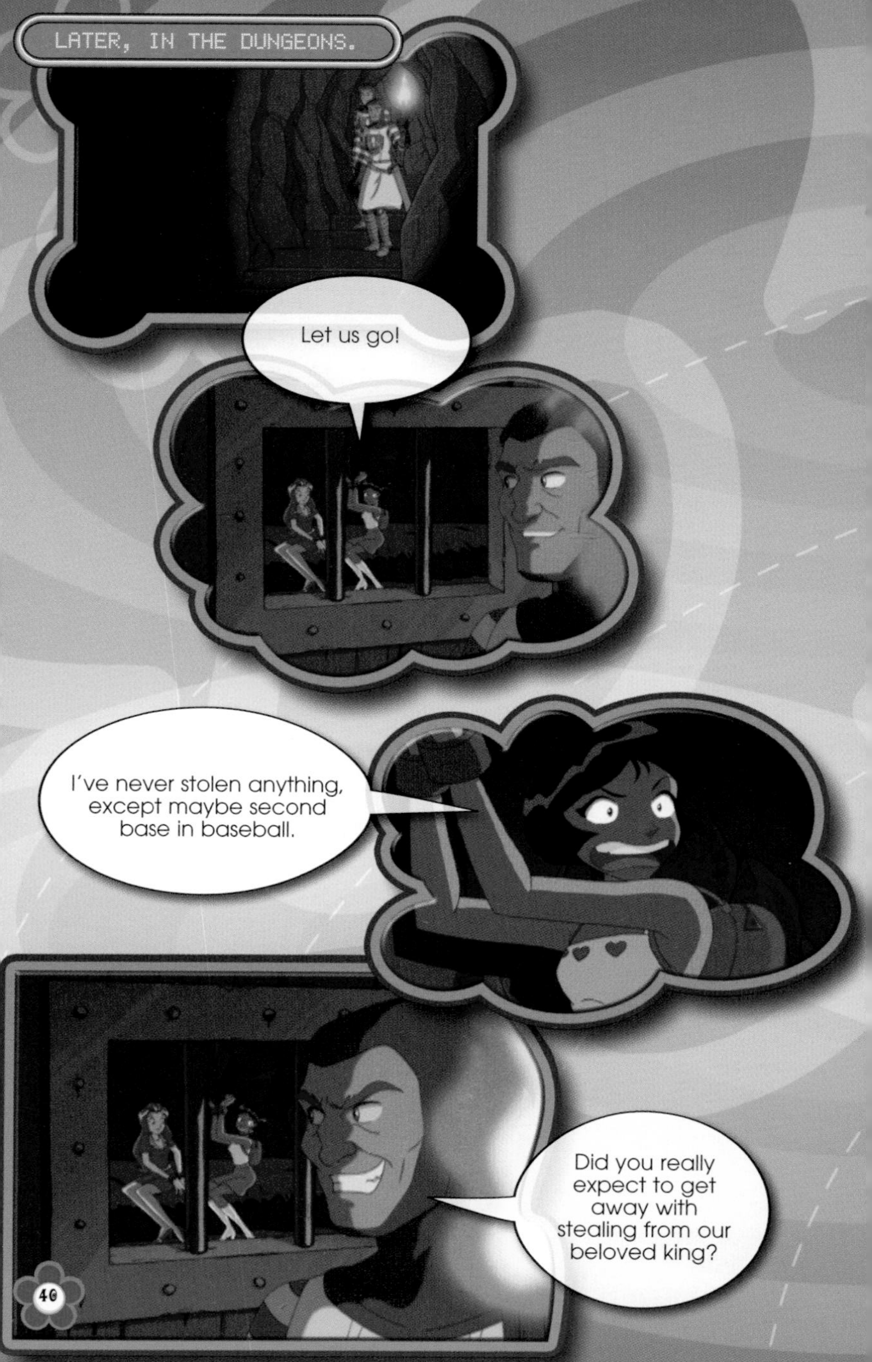
LATER, IN THE DUNGEONS.
Let us go!
I've never stolen anything, except maybe second base in baseball.
Did you really expect to get away with stealing from our beloved king?

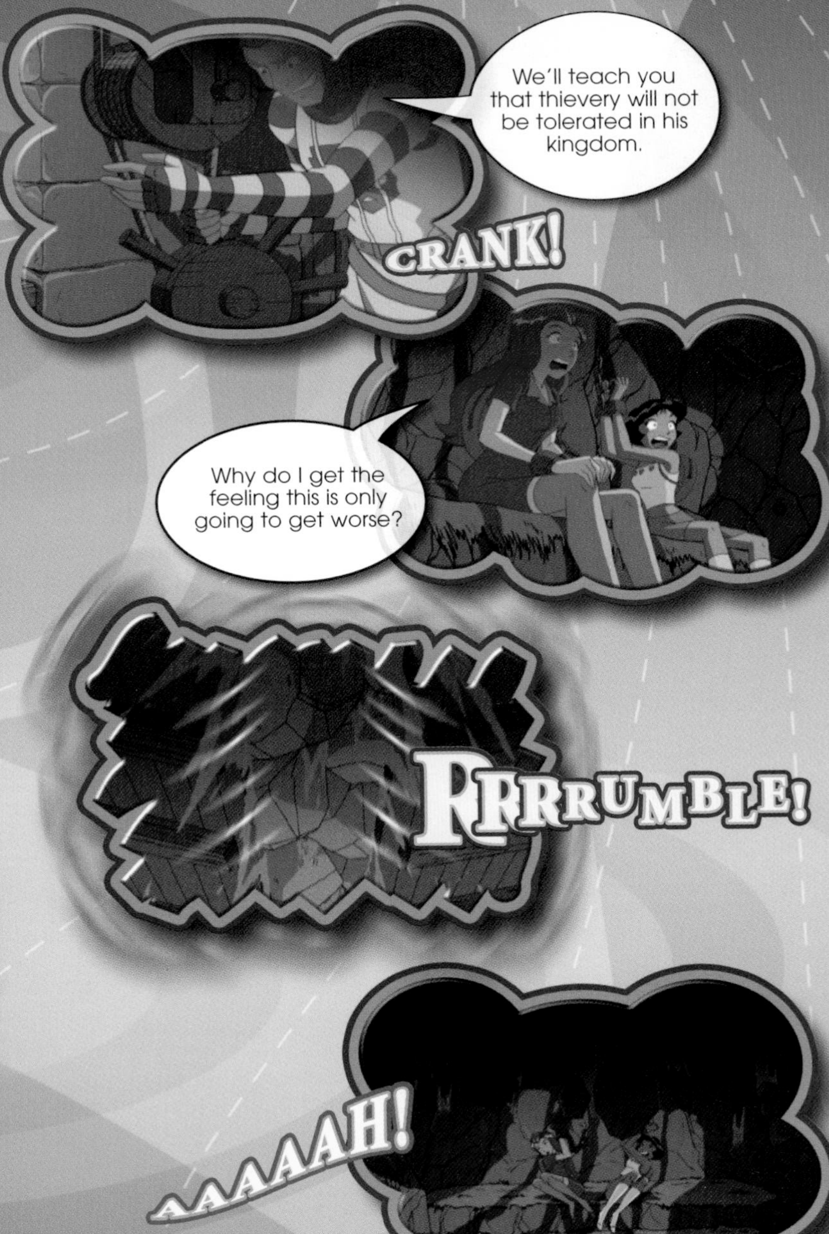
We'll teach you that thievery will not be tolerated in his kingdom.
CRANK!
Why do I get the feeling this is only going to get worse?
RRRRUMBLE!
AAAAAH!

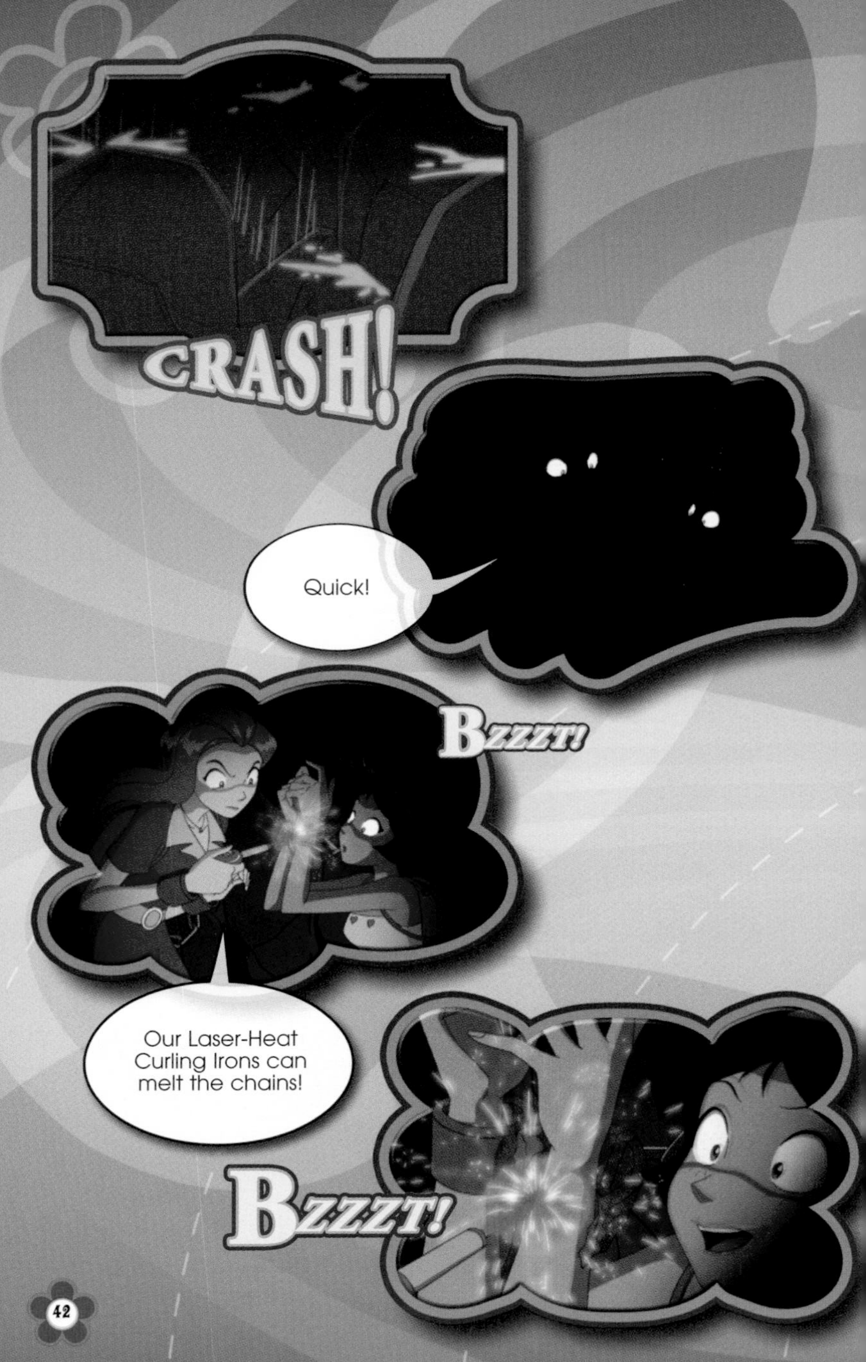
CRASH!
Quick!
Bzzzt!
Our Laser-Heat Curling Irons can melt the chains!
Bzzzt!

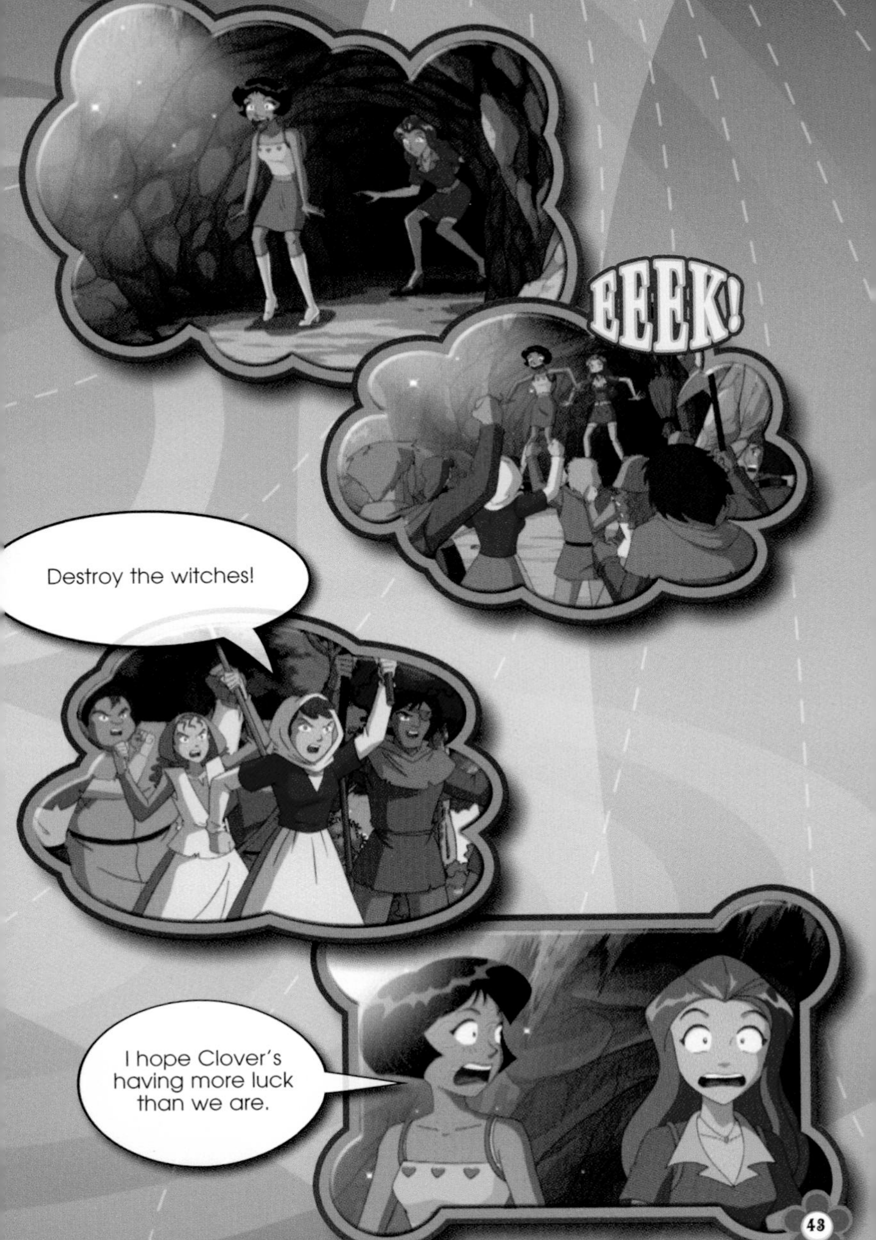
EEEK!
Destroy the witches!
I hope Clover's having more luck than we are.

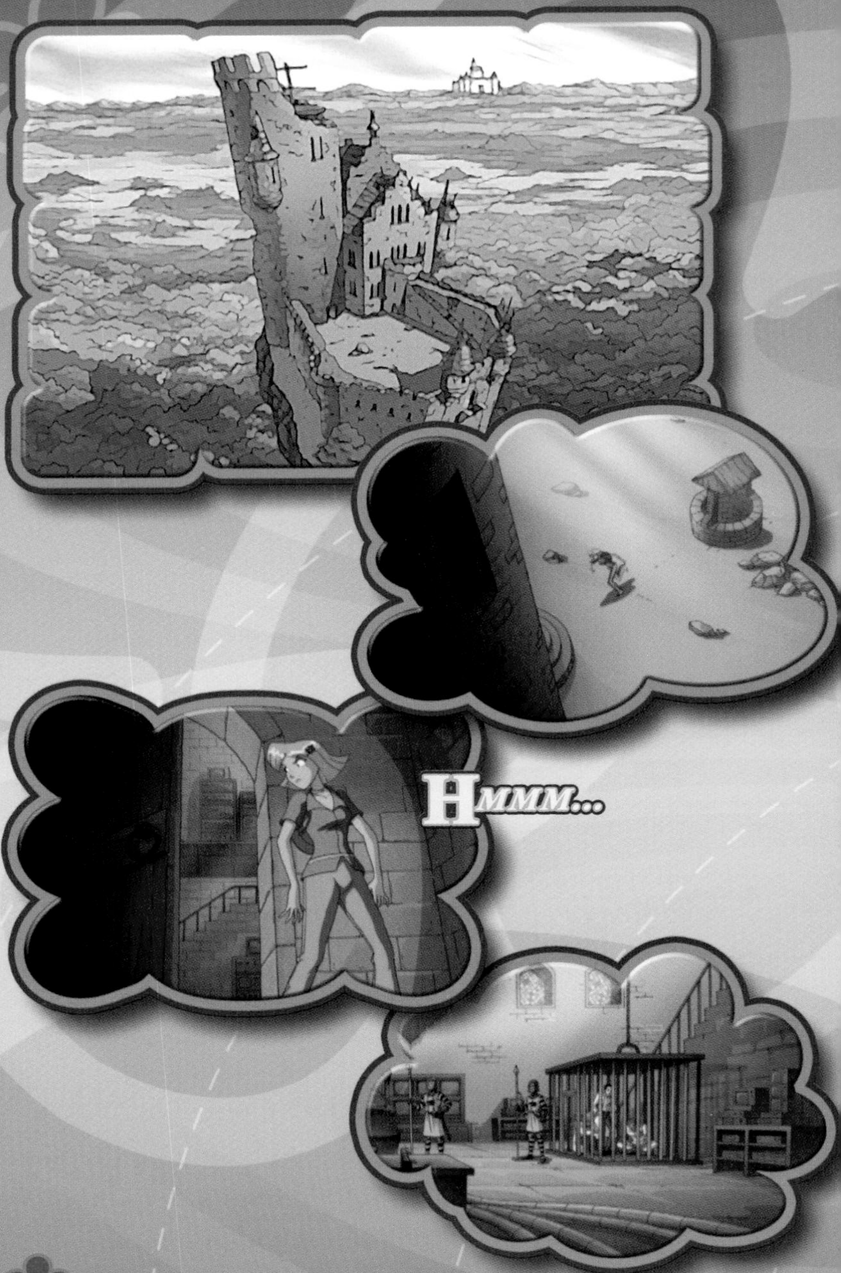
HMMM...

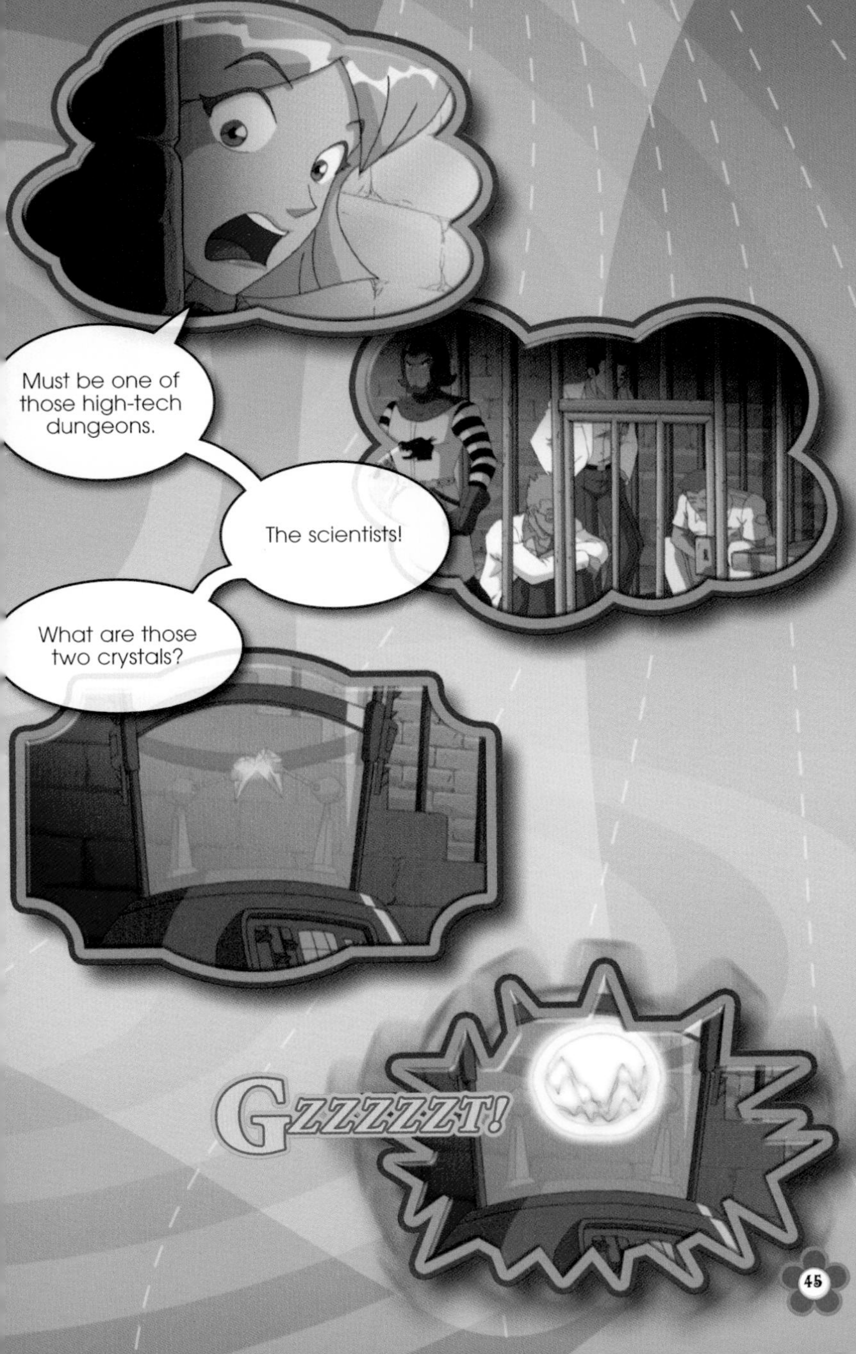

Must be one of those high-tech dungeons.
The scientists!
What are those two crystals?
GZZZZZT!

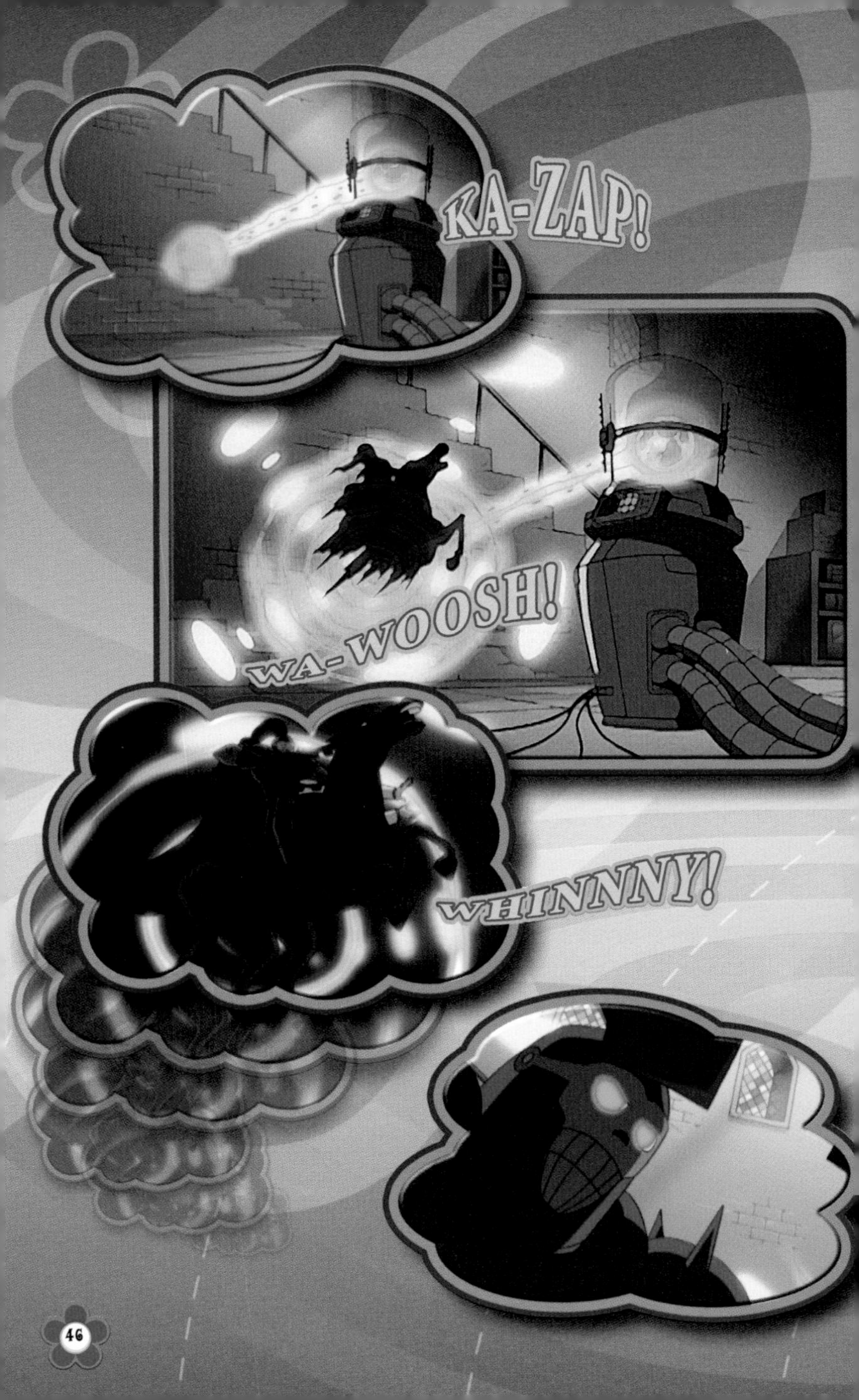
KA-ZAP!
WA-WOOSH!
WHINNNY!

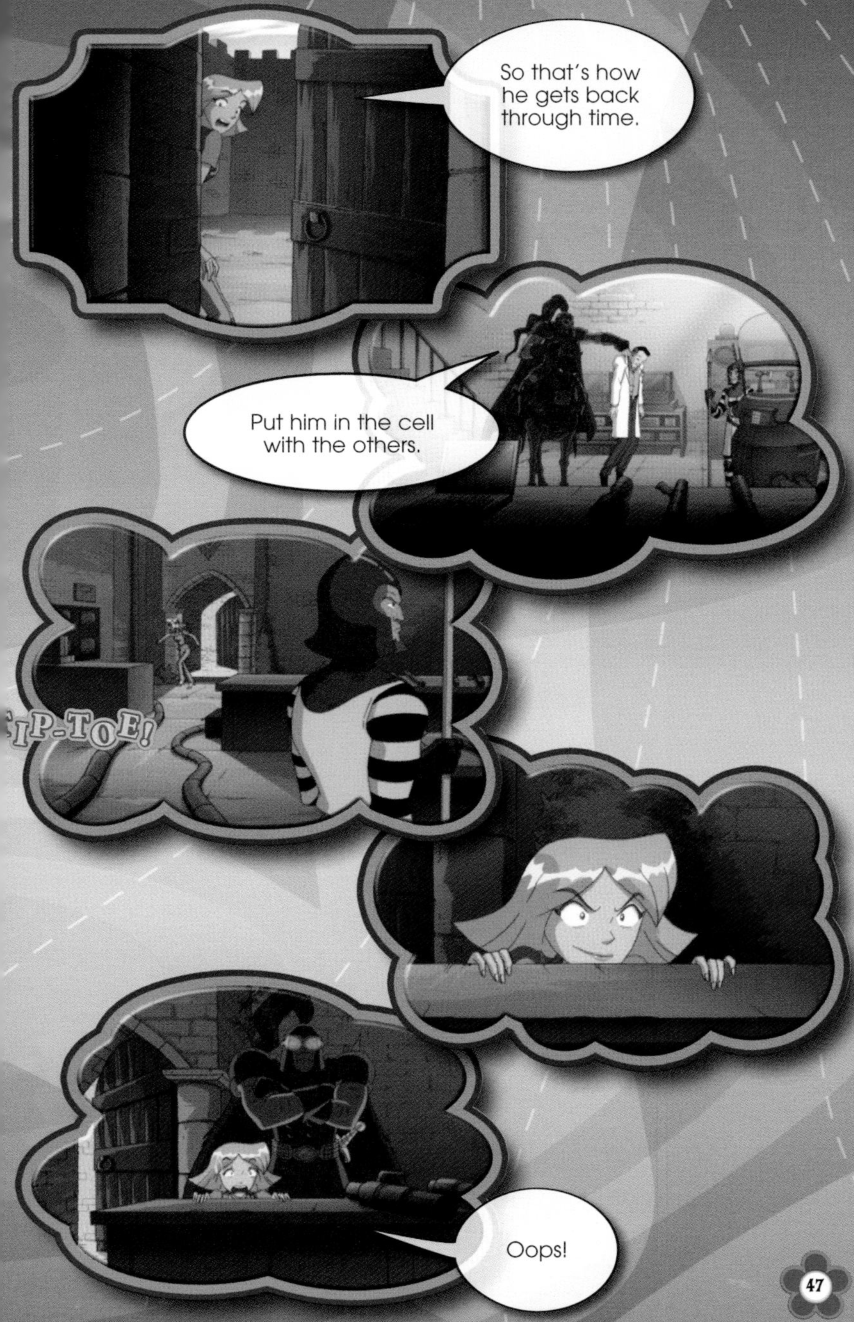
So that's how he gets back through time.
Put him in the cell with the others.
TIP-TOE!
Oops!

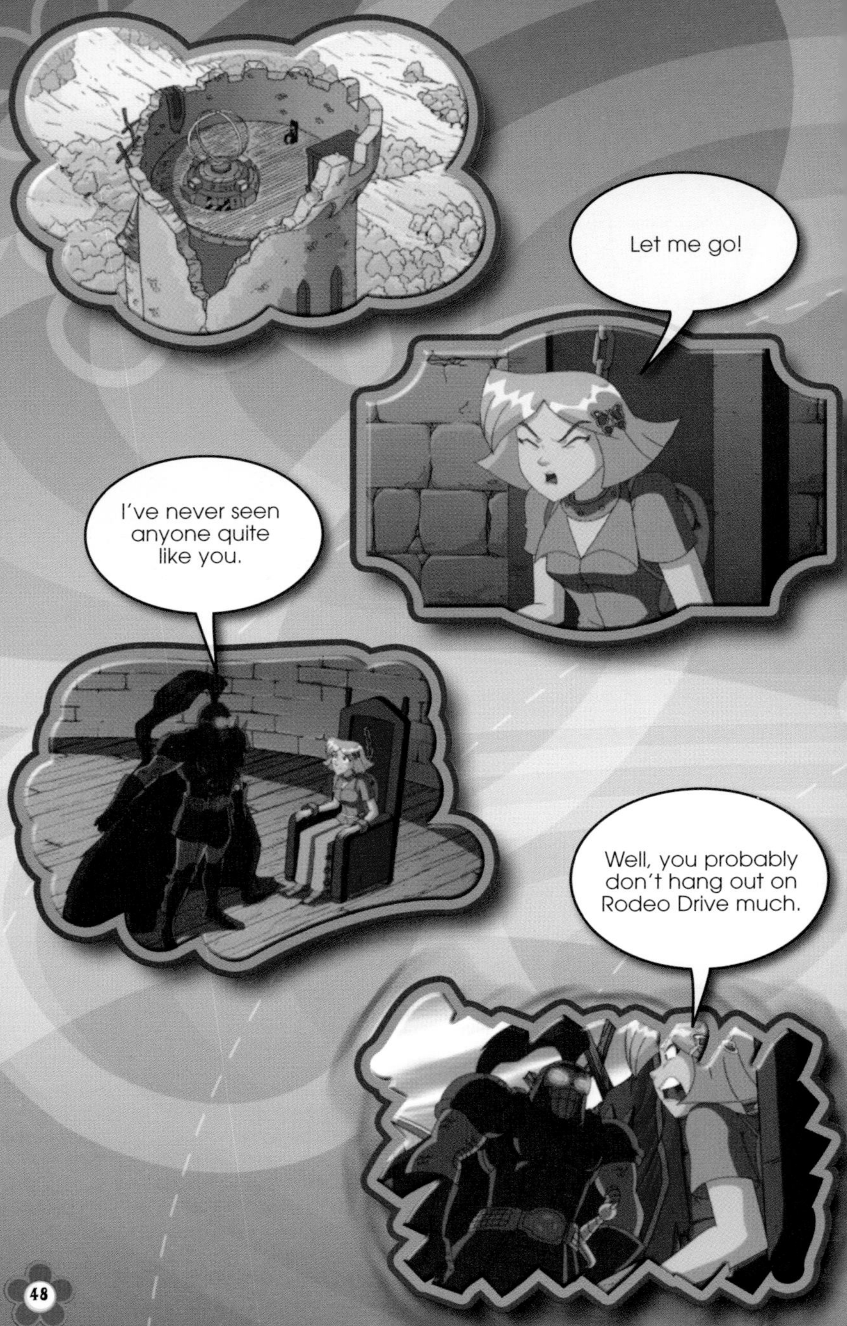
Let me go!
I've never seen anyone quite like you.
Well, you probably don't hang out on Rodeo Drive much.

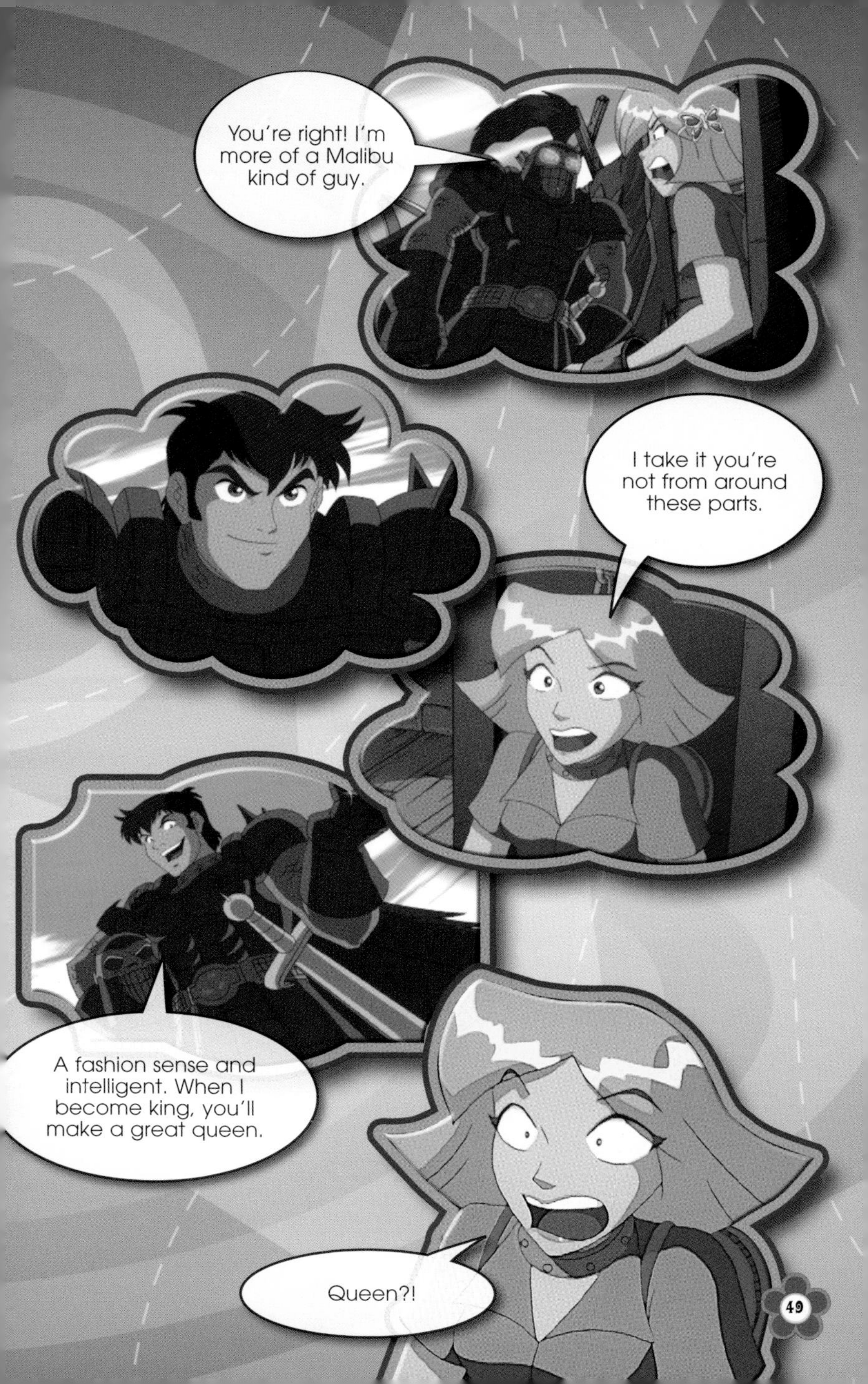
You're right! I'm more of a Malibu kind of guy.
I take it you're not from around these parts.
A fashion sense and intelligent. When I become king, you'll make a great queen.
Queen?!

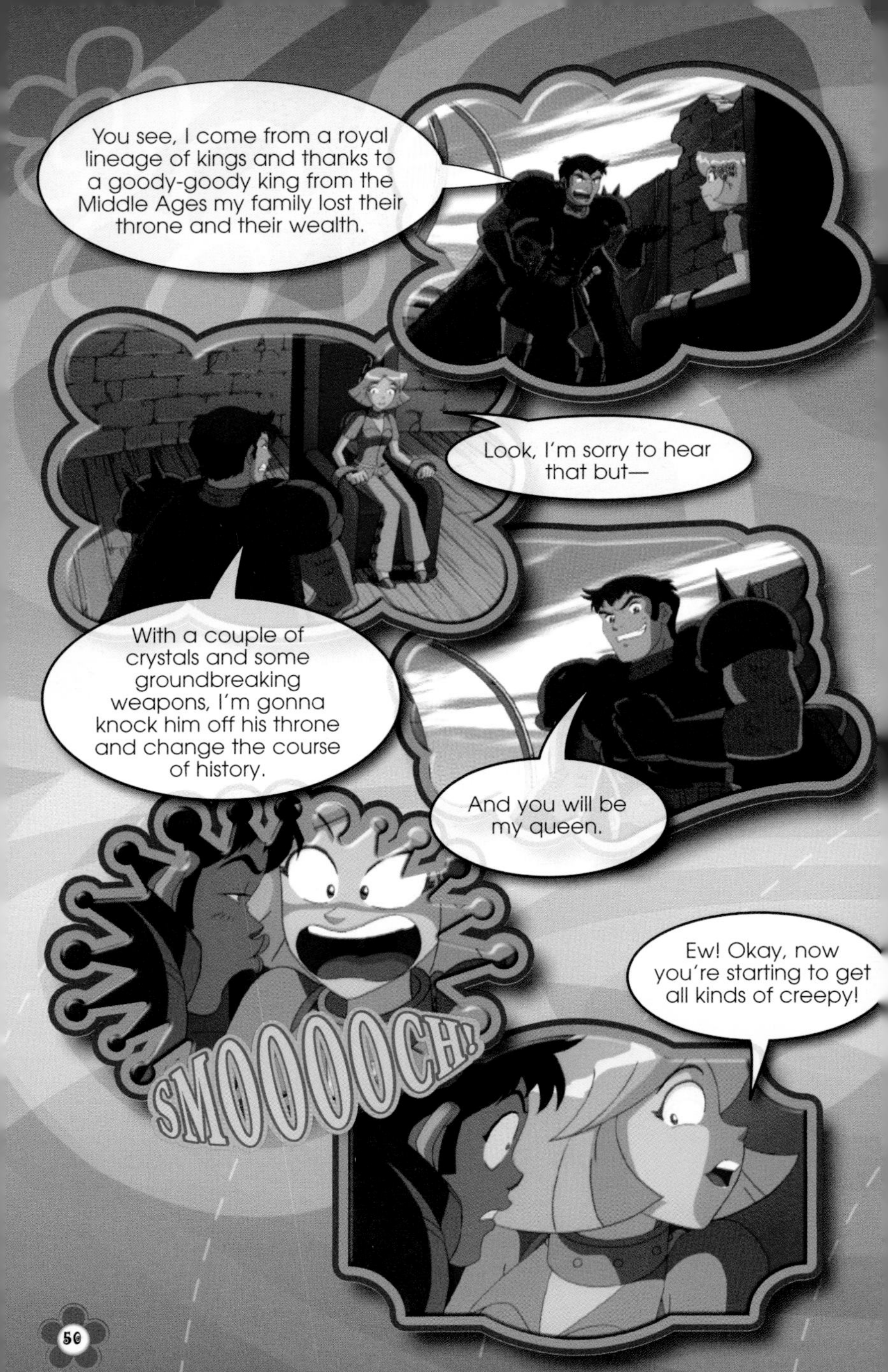
You see, I come from a royal lineage of kings and thanks to a goody-goody king from the Middle Ages my family lost their throne and their wealth.
Look, I'm sorry to hear that but—
With a couple of crystals and some groundbreaking weapons, I'm gonna knock him off his throne and change the course of history.
And you will be my queen.
SMOOOOOCH!
Ew! Okay, now you're starting to get all kinds of creepy!

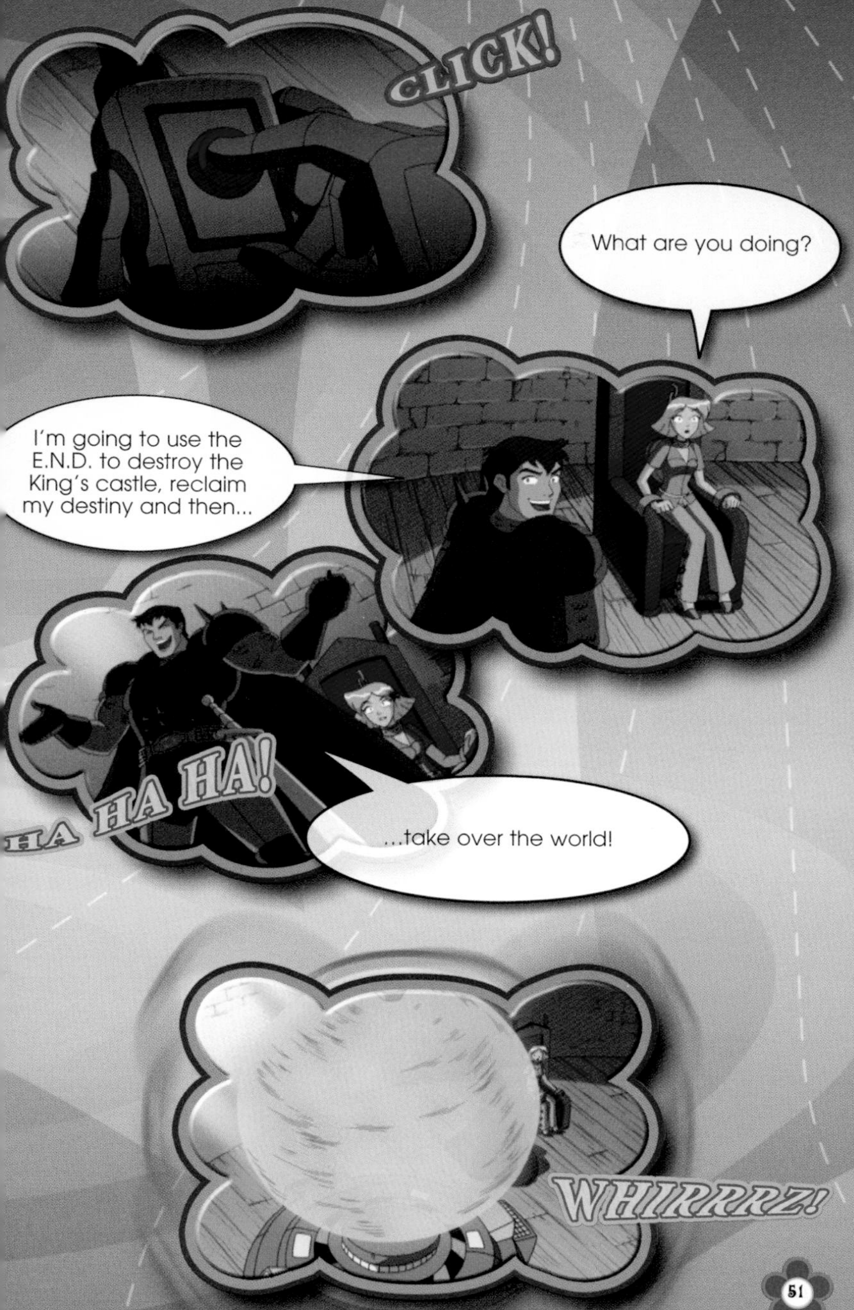
CLICK!
What are you doing?
I'm going to use the E.N.D. to destroy the King's castle, reclaim my destiny and then...
HA HA HA!
...take over the world!
WHIRRRZ!

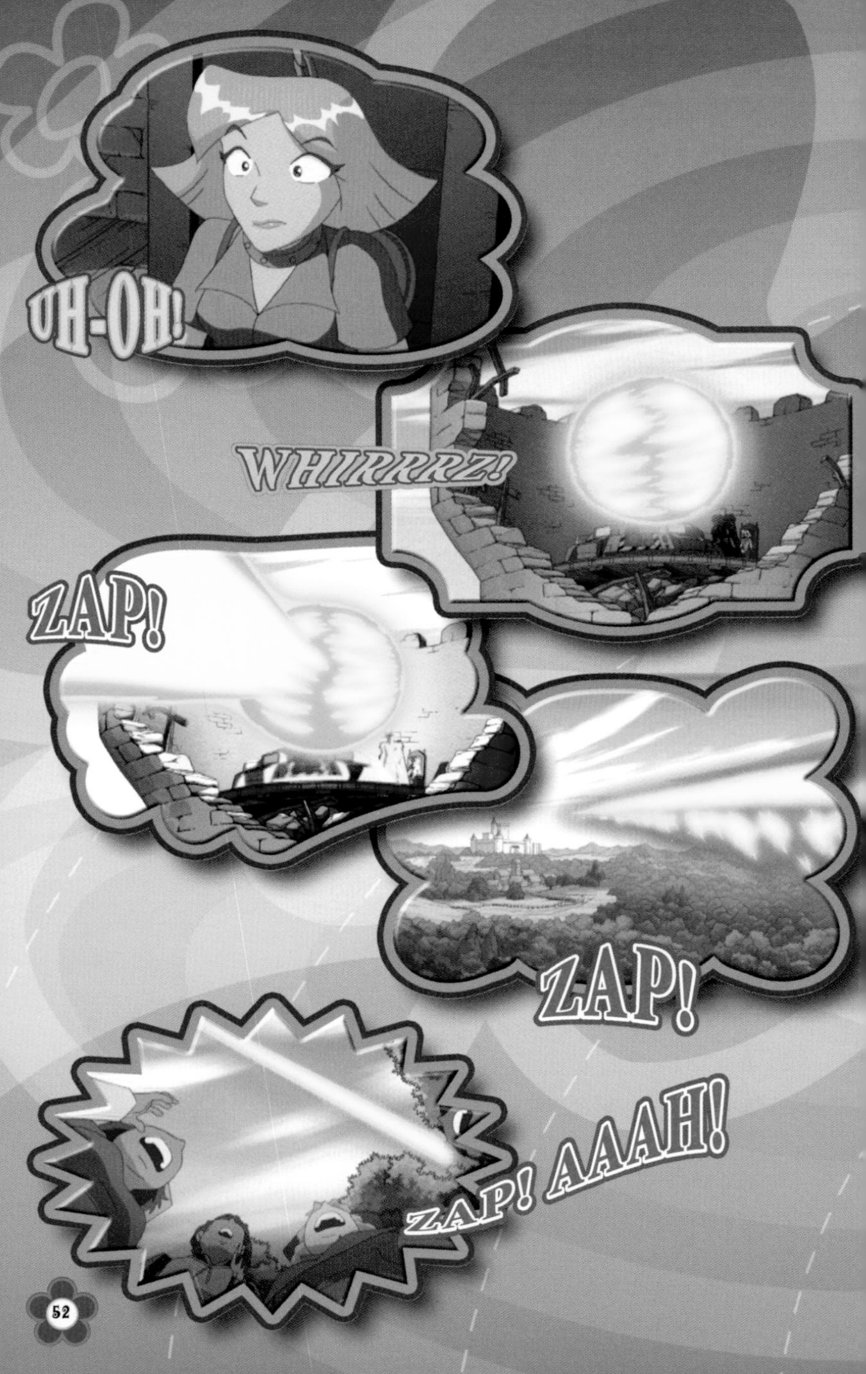
UH-OH!
WHIRRRZ!
ZAP!
ZAP!
ZAP! AAAH!

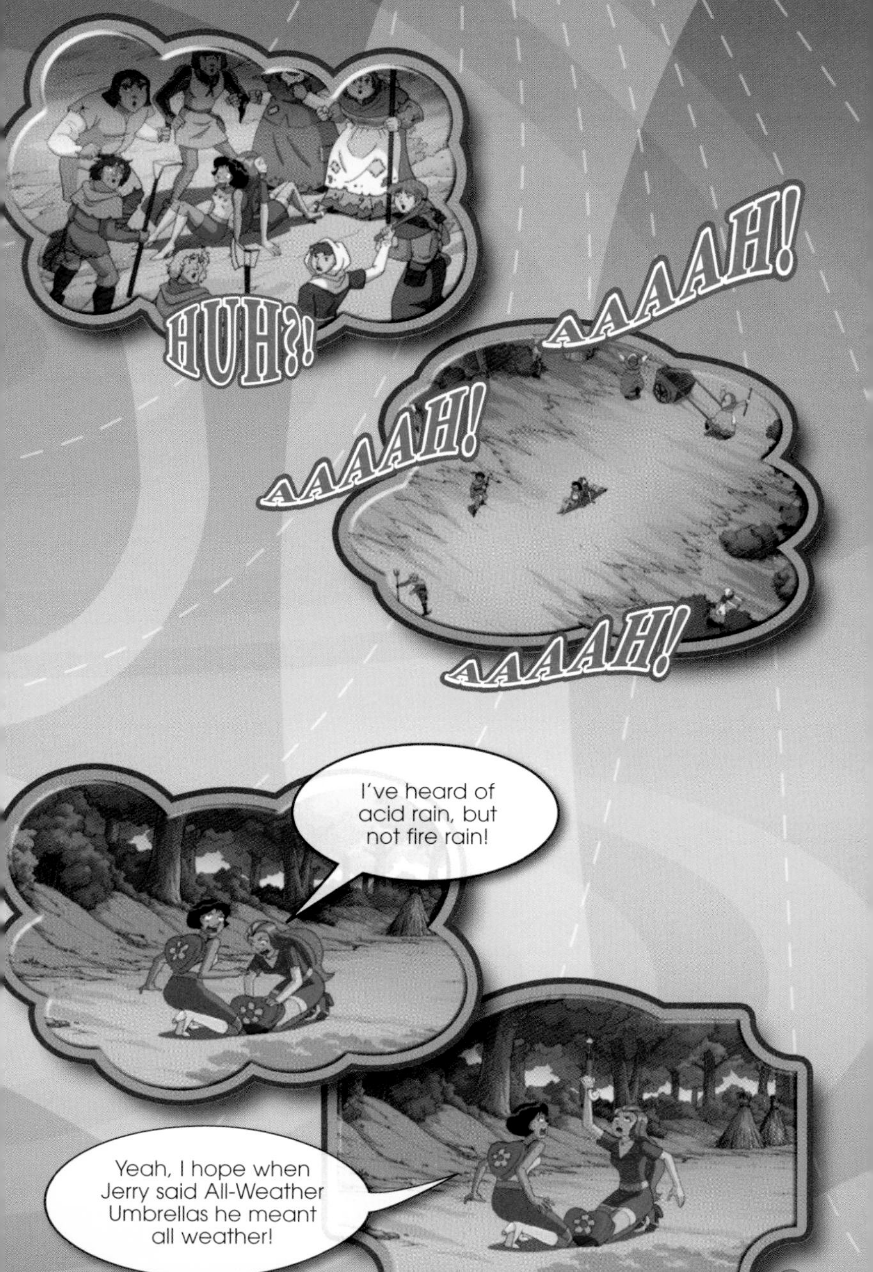
HUH?!
AAAAAH!
AAAAAH!
AAAAAH!
I've heard of acid rain, but not fire rain!
Yeah, I hope when Jerry said All-Weather Umbrellas he meant all weather!

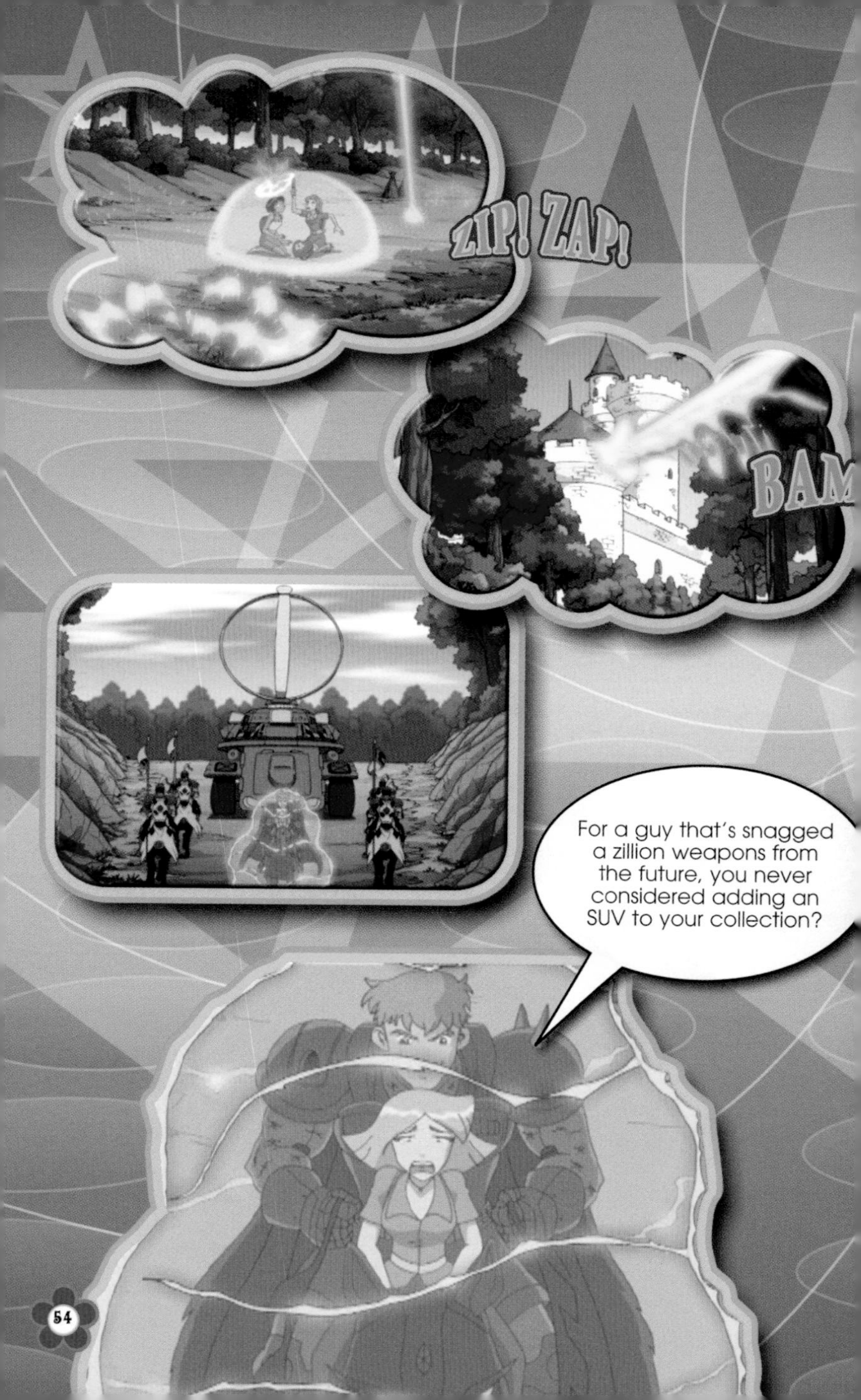
ZIP! ZAP!
BAM
For a guy that's snagged a zillion weapons from the future, you never considered adding an SUV to your collection?

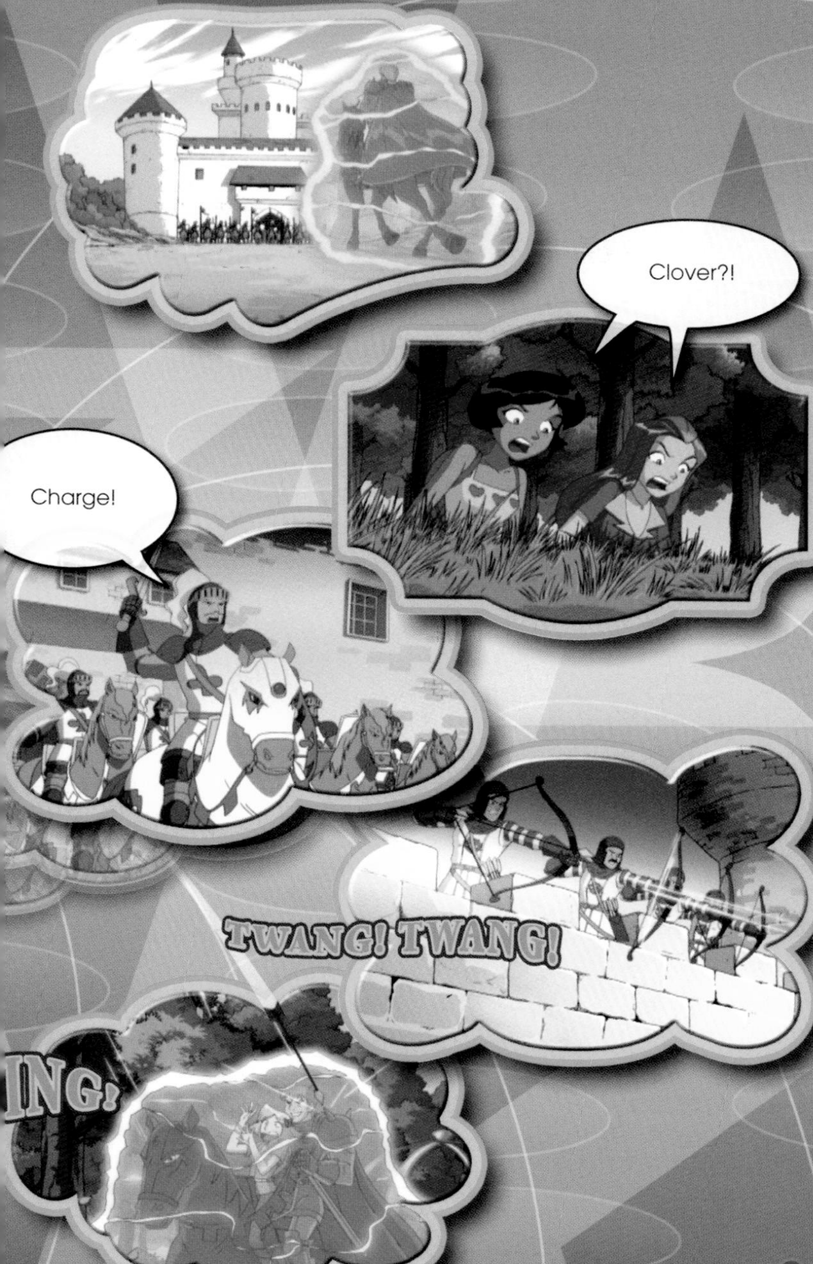
Clover?!
Charge!
TWANG! TWANG!
ING!

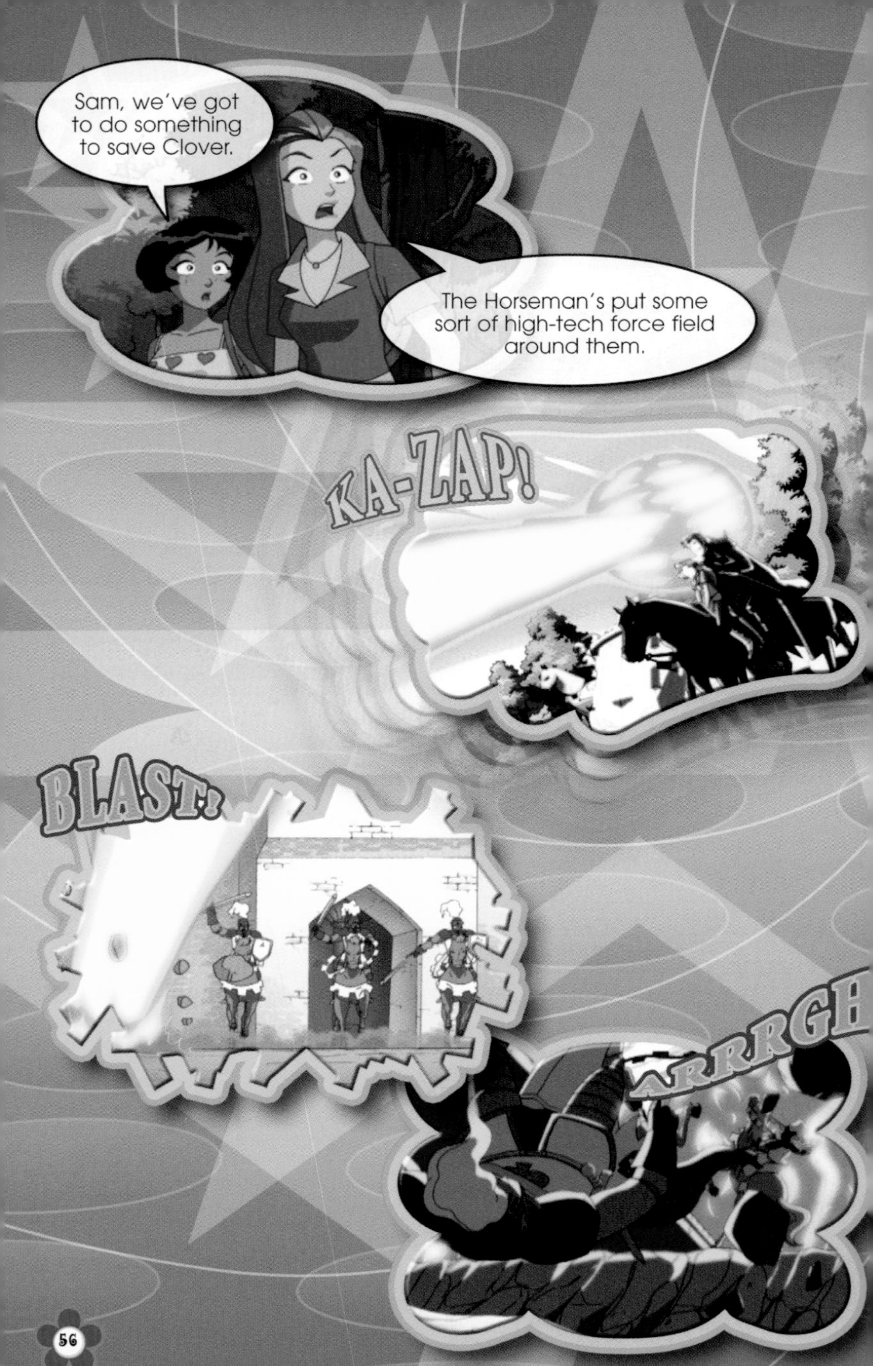
Sam, we've got to do something to save Clover.
The Horseman's put some sort of high-tech force field around them.
KA-ZAP!
BLAST!
ARRRGH

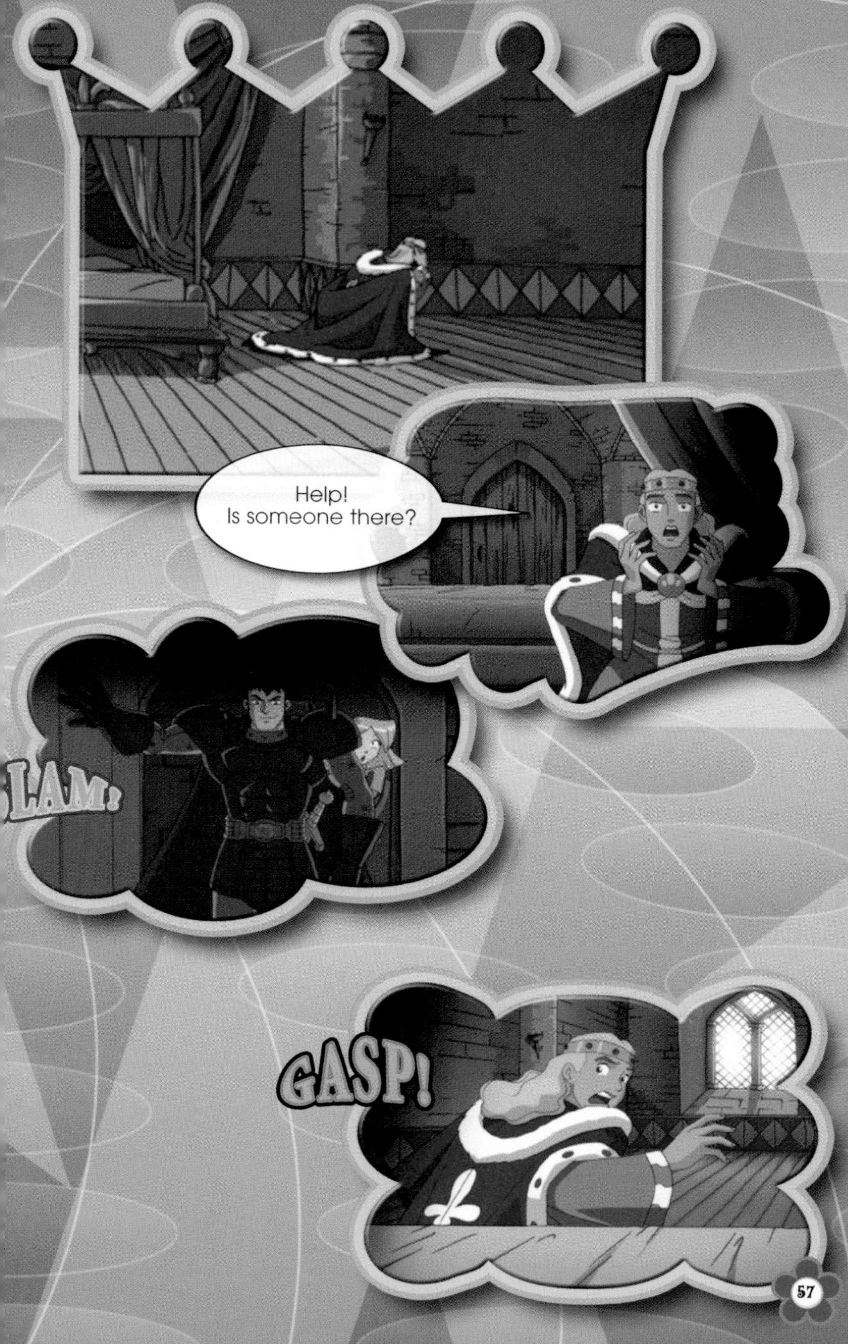
Help!
Is someone there?
LAM!
GASP!

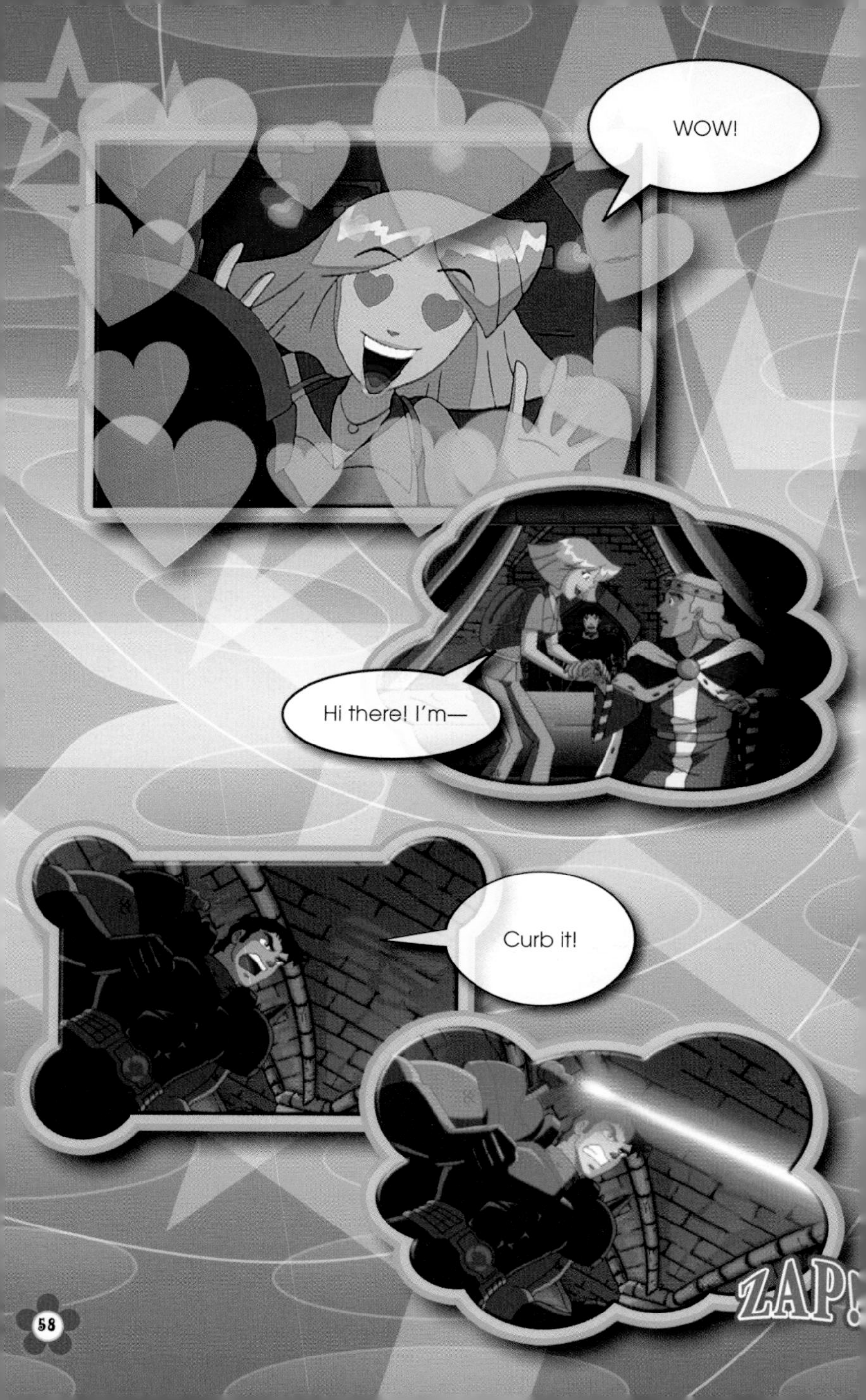
WOW!
Hi there! I'm—
Curb it!
ZAP!

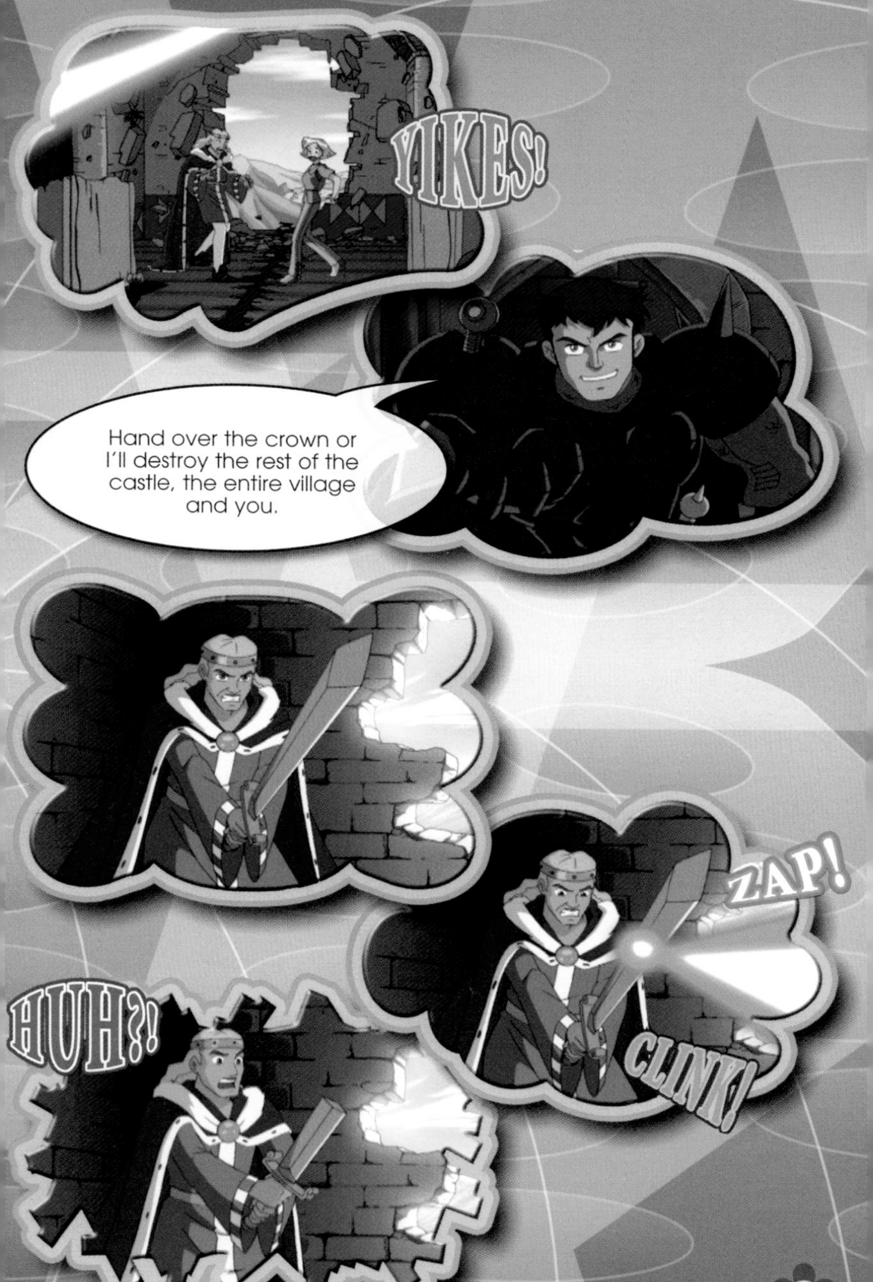
YIKES!
Hand over the crown or I'll destroy the rest of the castle, the entire village and you.
ZAP!
CLINK!
HUH?!

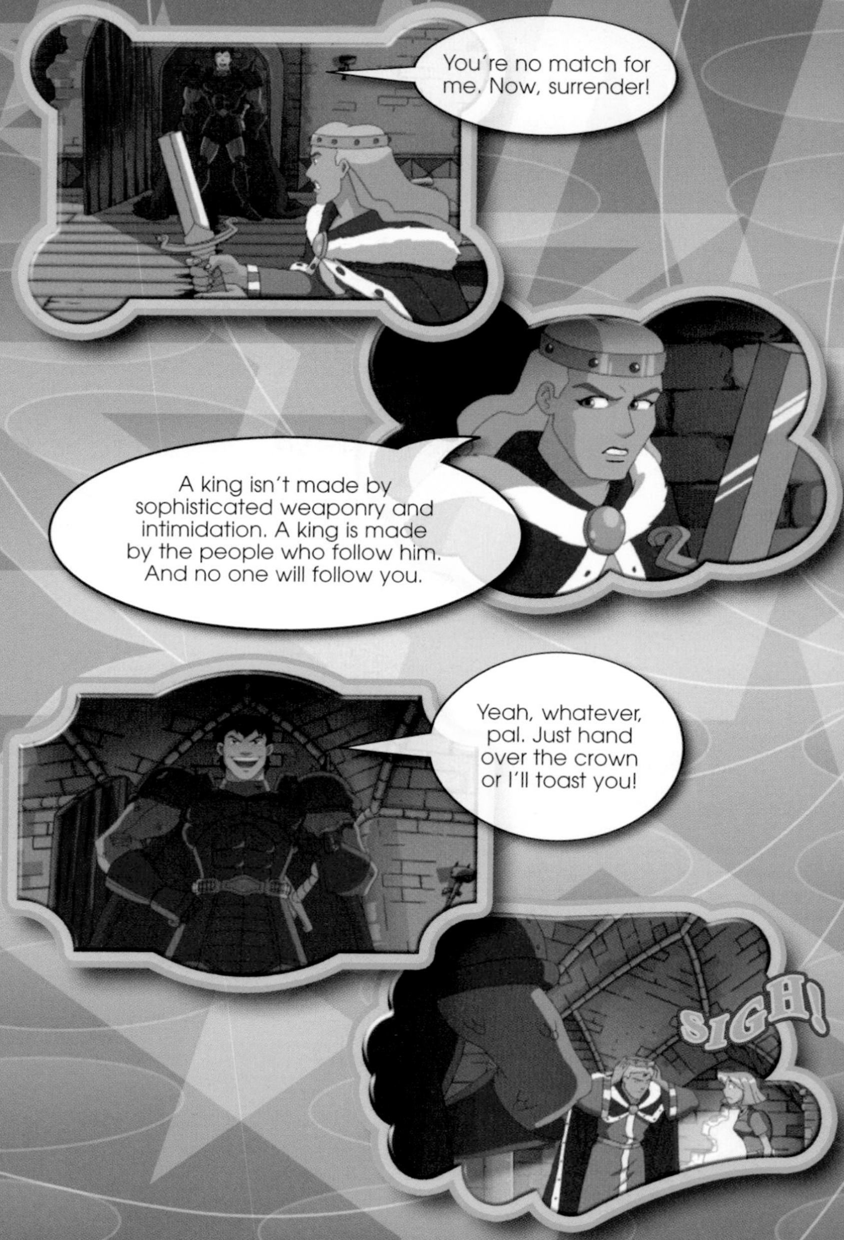
You're no match for me. Now, surrender!
A king isn't made by sophisticated weaponry and intimidation. A king is made by the people who follow him. And no one will follow you.
Yeah, whatever, pal. Just hand over the crown or I'll toast you!
SIGH!

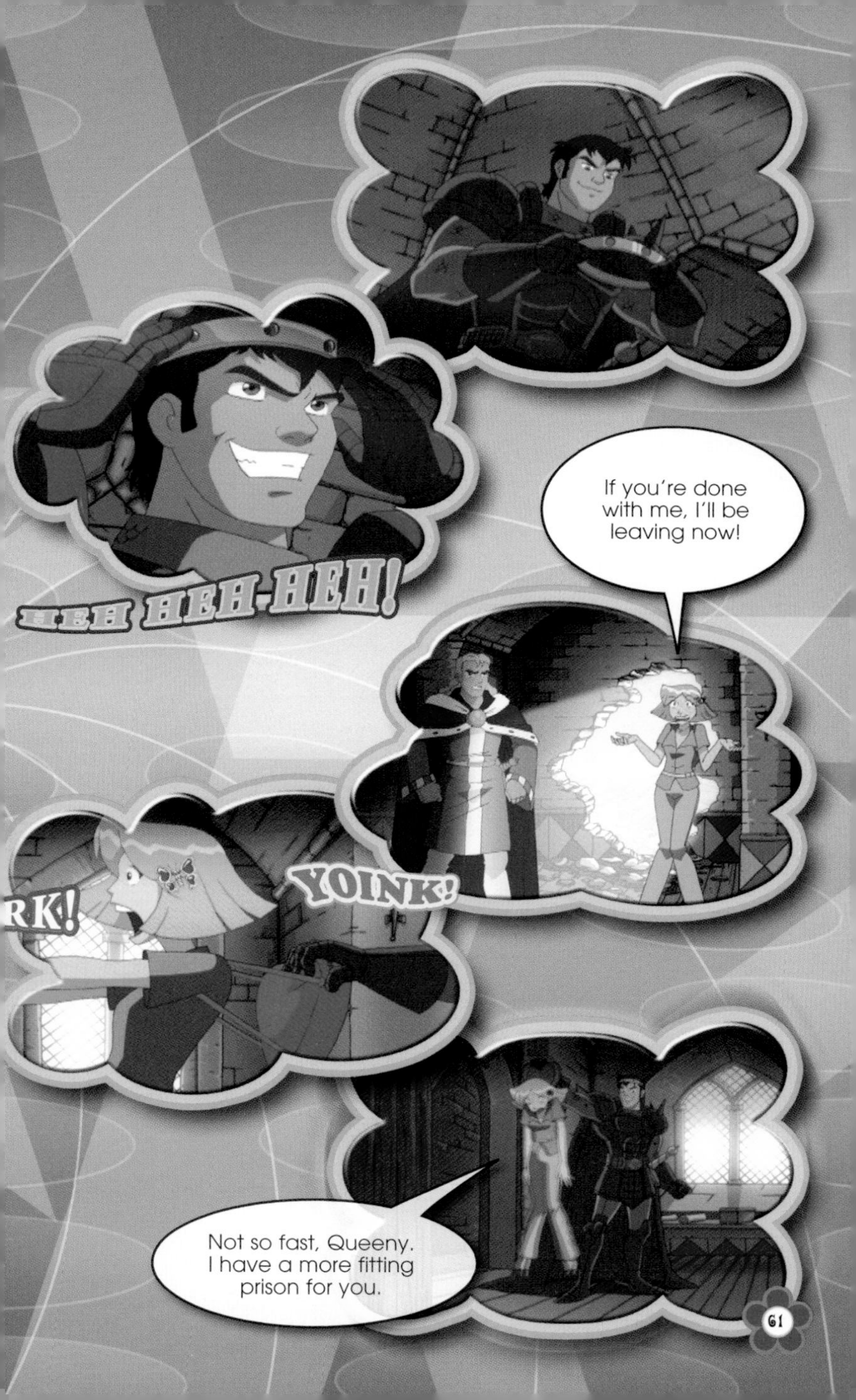
HEH HEH HEH!
If you're done with me, I'll be leaving now!
YOINK!
RK!
Not so fast, Queeny. I have a more fitting prison for you.

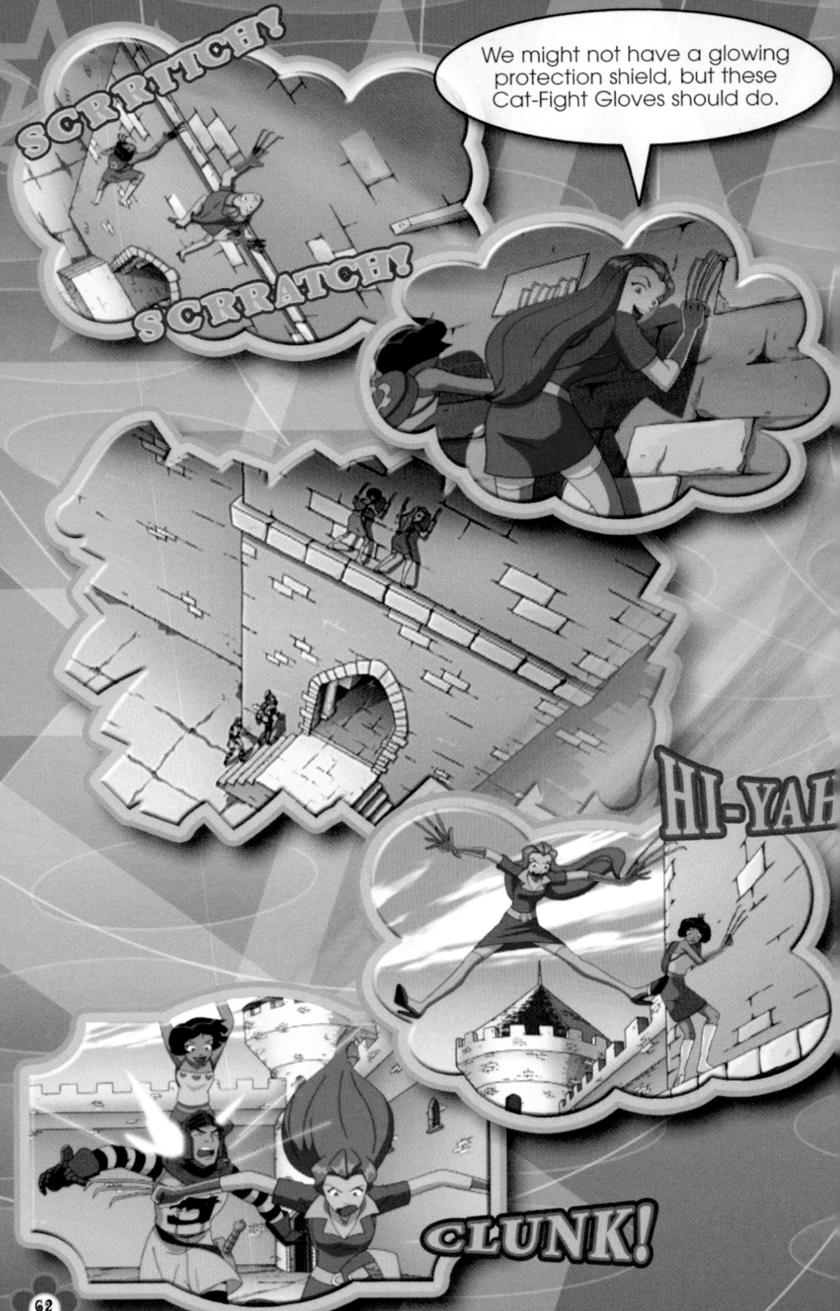
SCRRITCH!
We might not have a glowing protection shield, but these Cat-Fight Gloves should do.
SCRRATCH!
HI-YAH
CLUNK!

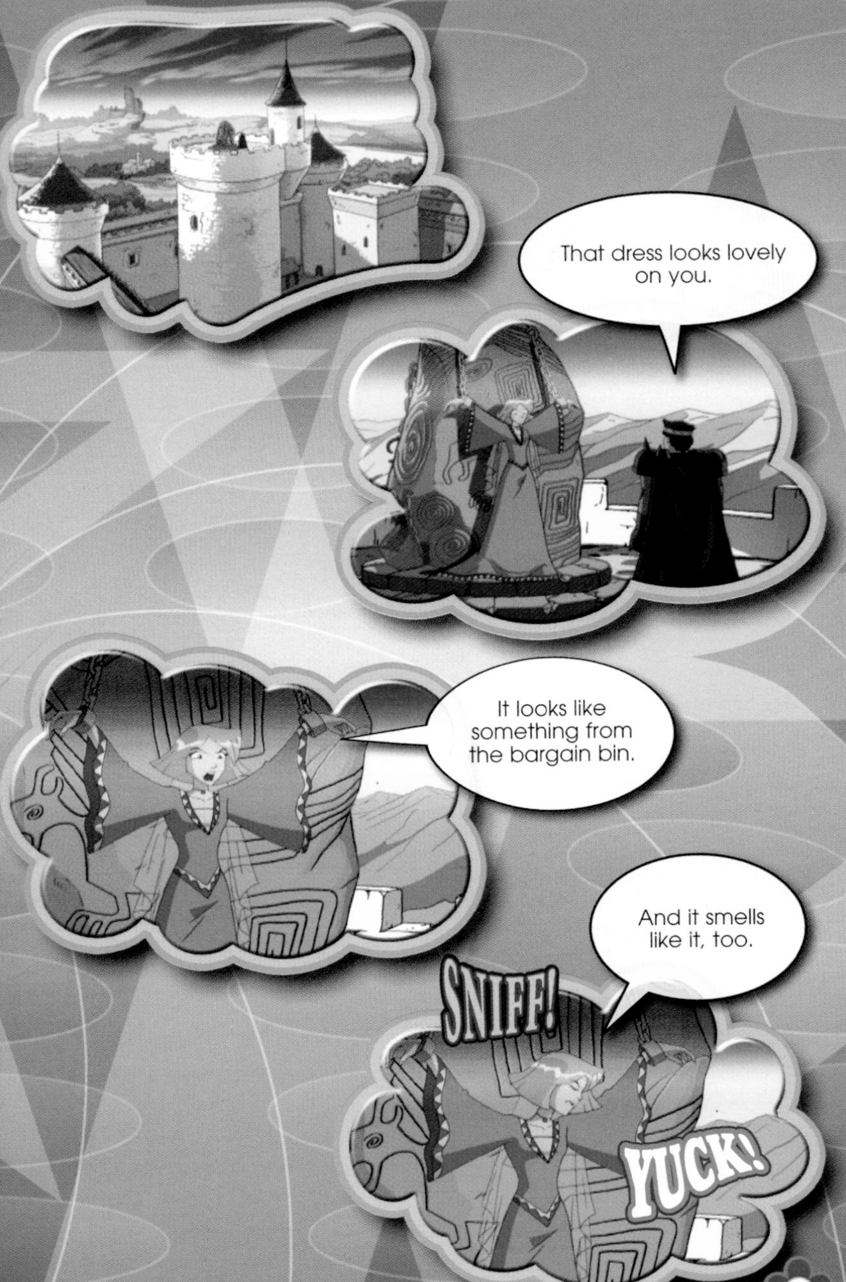
That dress looks lovely on you.
It looks like something from the bargain bin.
And it smells like it, too.
SNIFF!
YUCK!

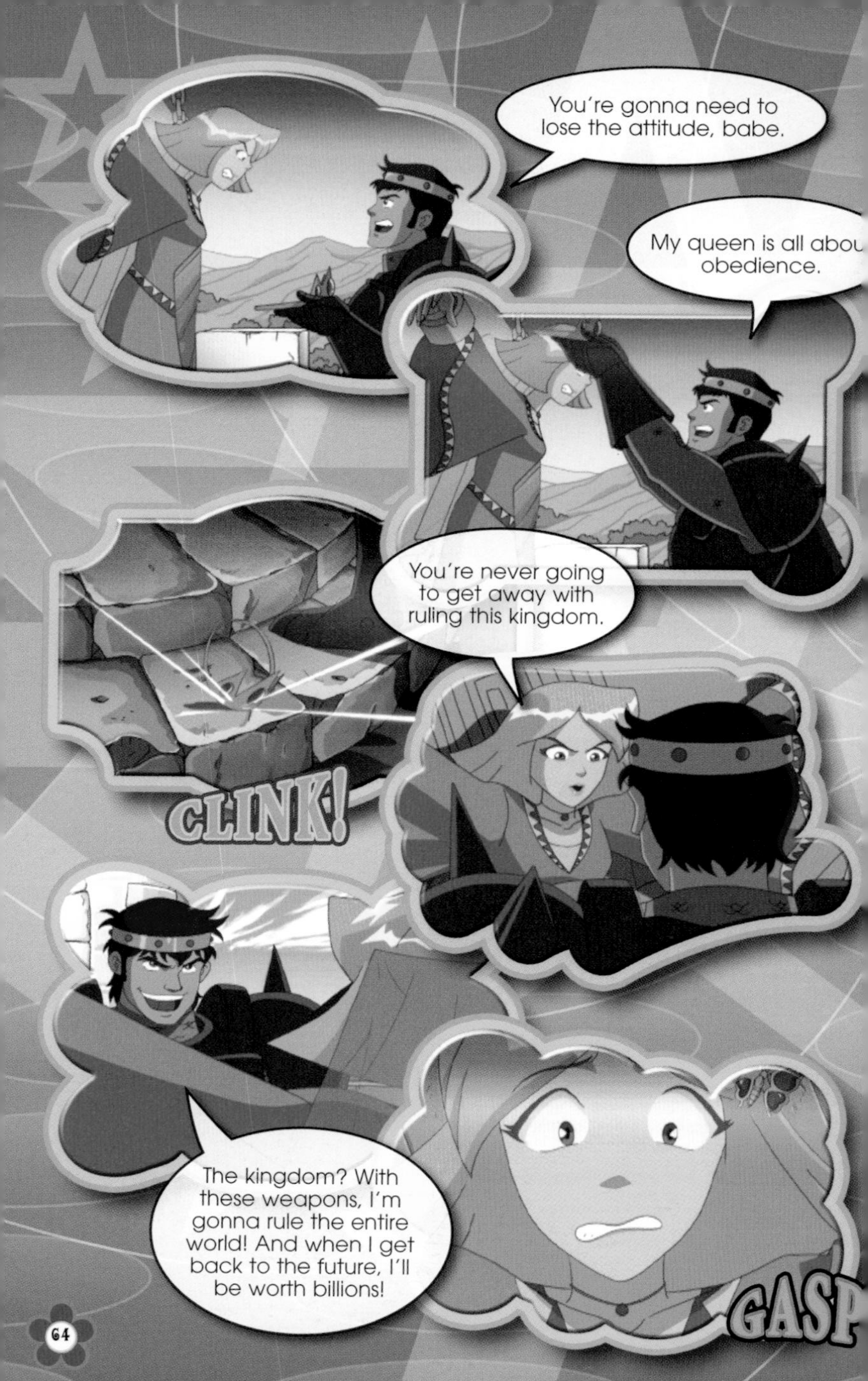
You're gonna need to lose the attitude, babe.
My queen is all abou obedience.
CLINK!
You're never going to get away with ruling this kingdom.
The kingdom? With these weapons, I'm gonna rule the entire world! And when I get back to the future, I'll be worth billions!
GASP

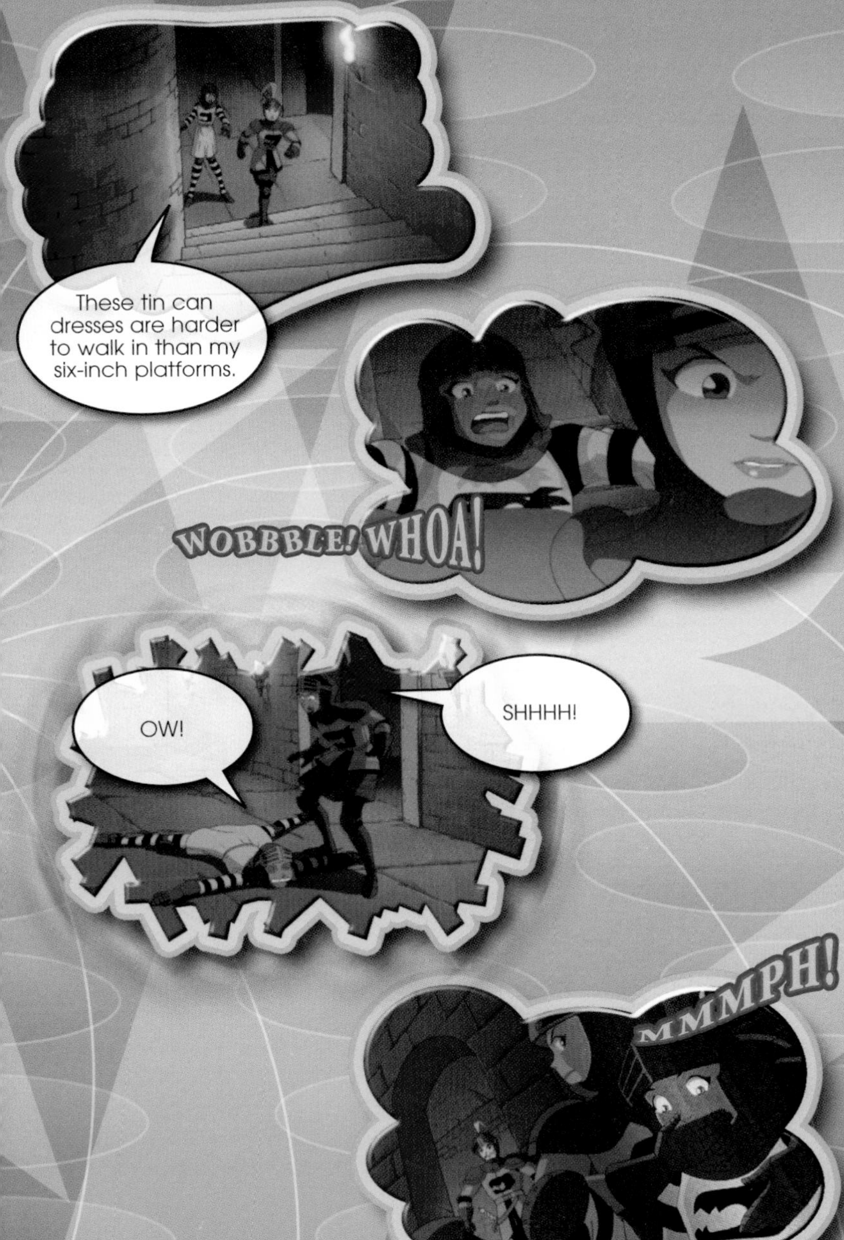
These tin can dresses are harder to walk in than my six-inch platforms.
WOBBBLE! WHOA!
OW!
SHHHH!
MMMPH!

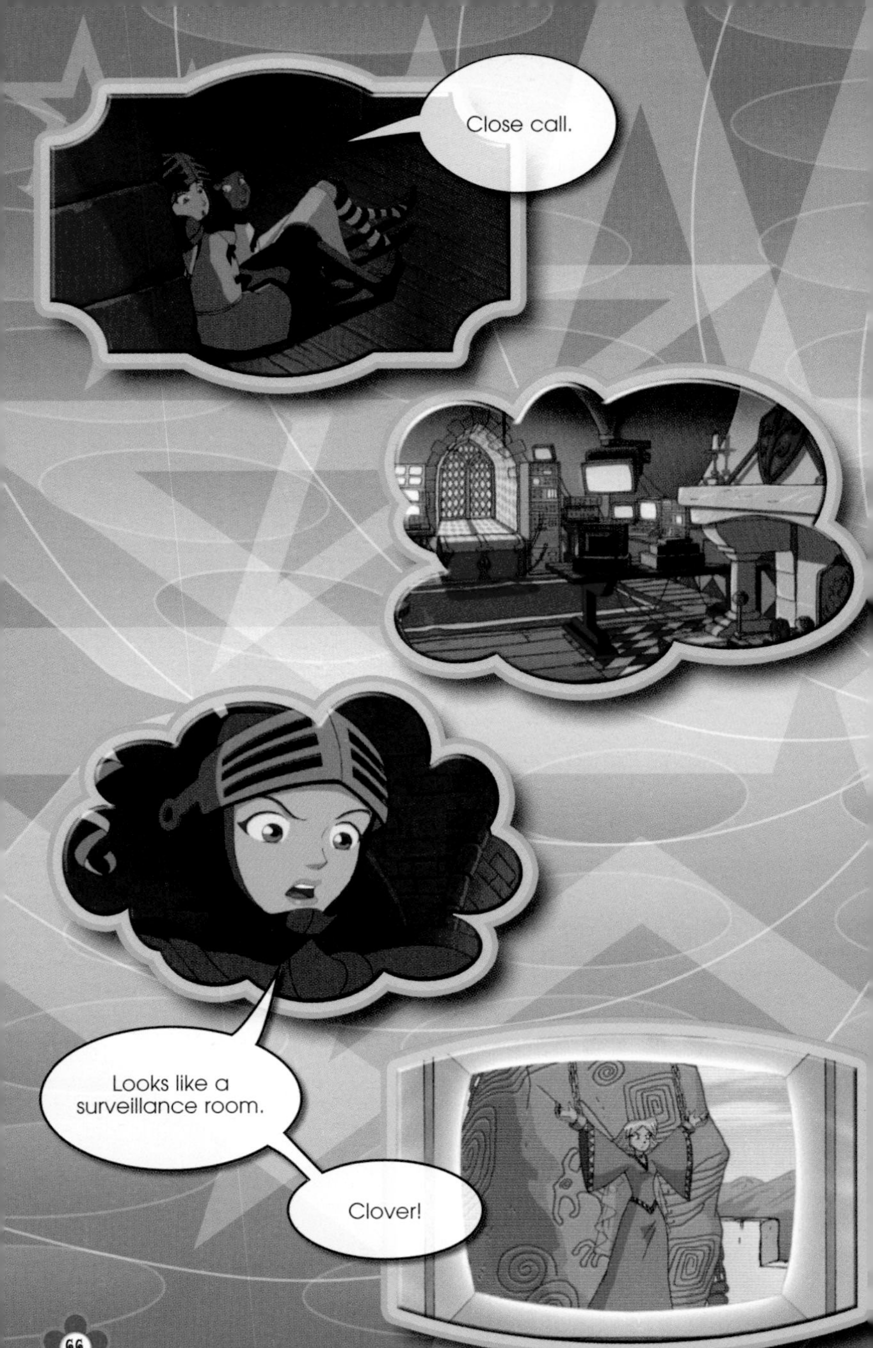
Close call.
Looks like a surveillance room.
Clover!

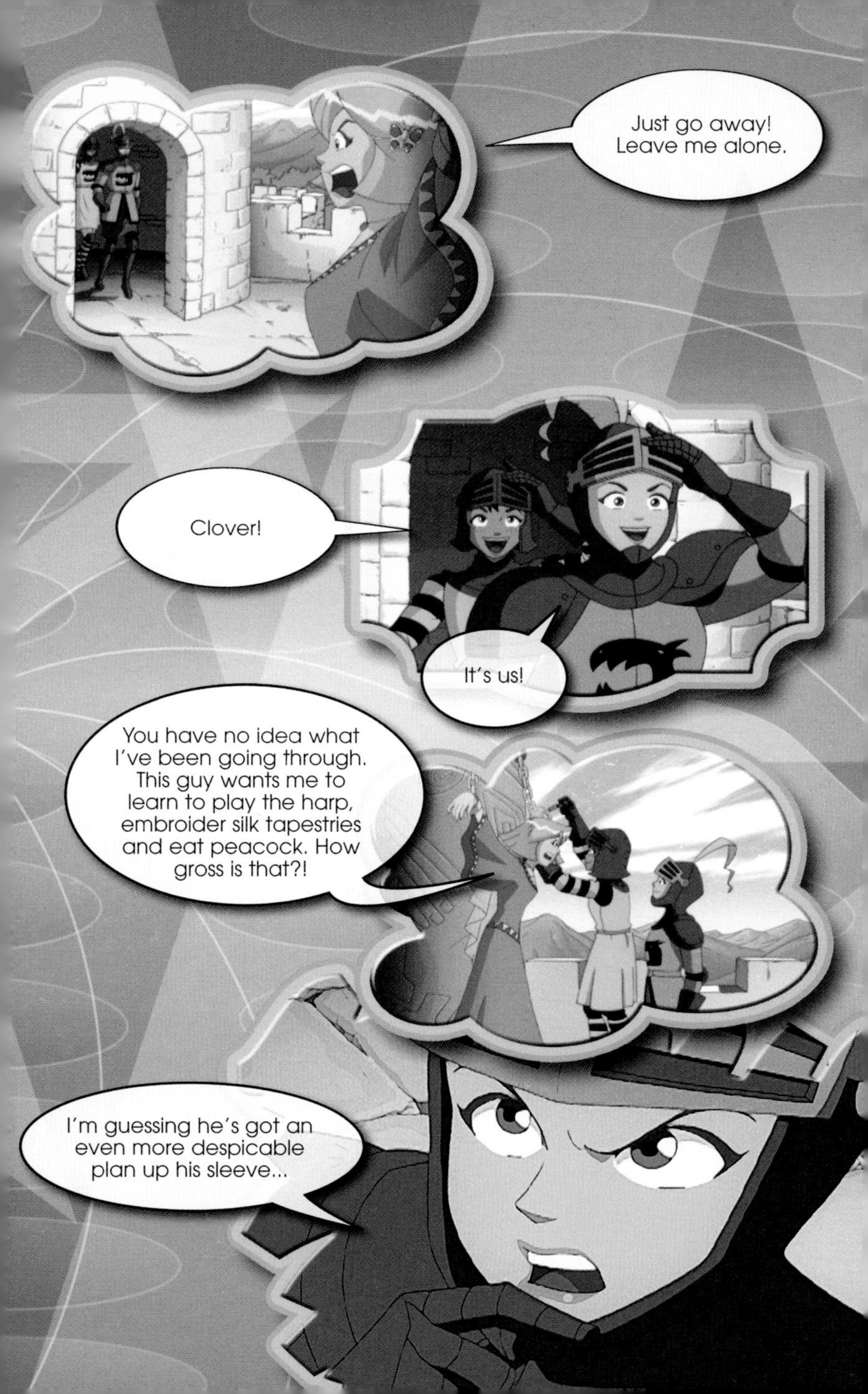
Just go away! Leave me alone.
Clover!
It's us!
You have no idea what I've been going through. This guy wants me to learn to play the harp, embroider silk tapestries and eat peacock. How gross is that?!
I'm guessing he's got an even more despicable plan up his sleeve...

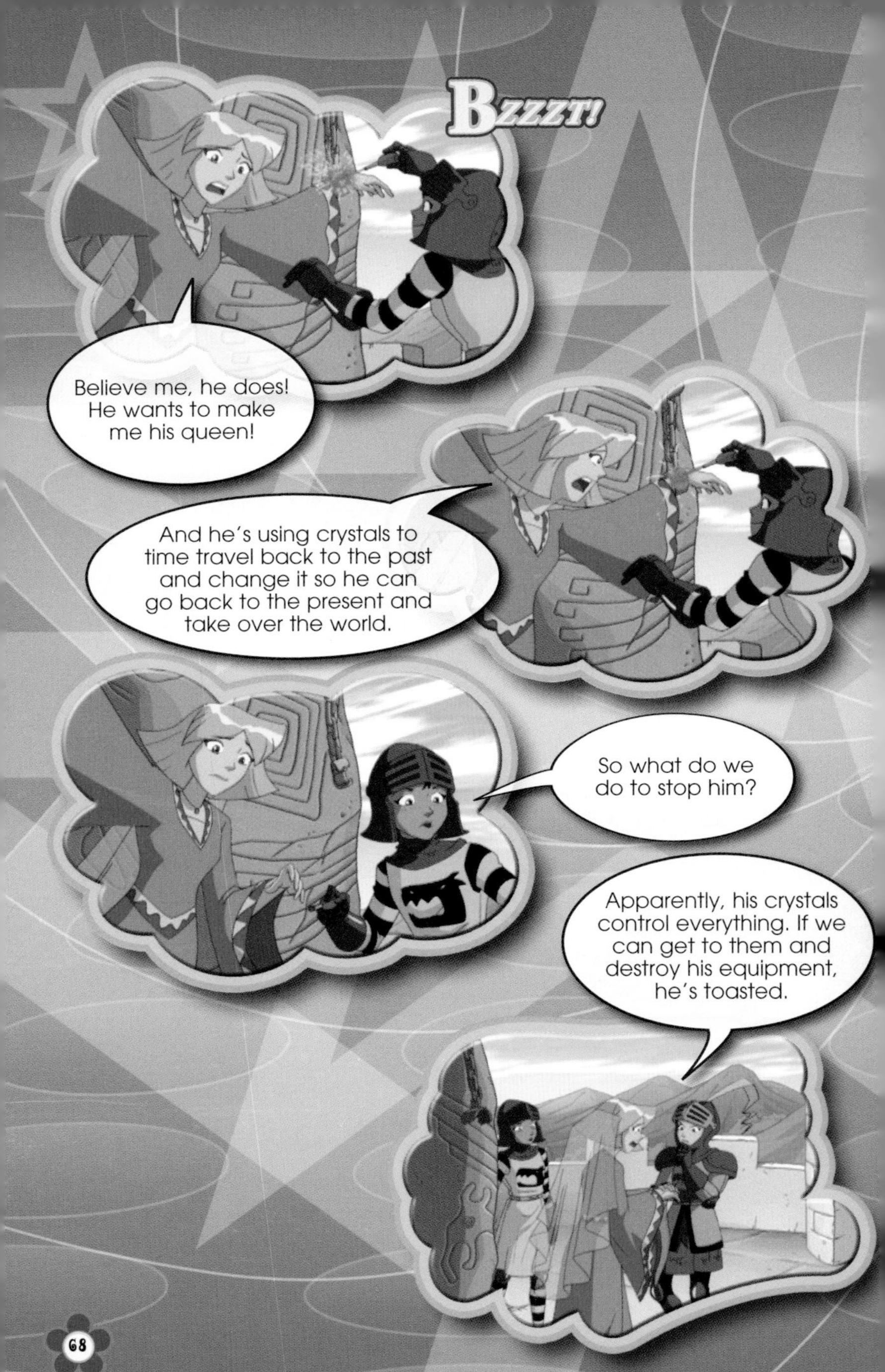
BZZZT!
Believe me, he does! He wants to make me his queen!
And he's using crystals to time travel back to the past and change it so he can go back to the present and take over the world.
So what do we do to stop him?
Apparently, his crystals control everything. If we can get to them and destroy his equipment, he's toasted.

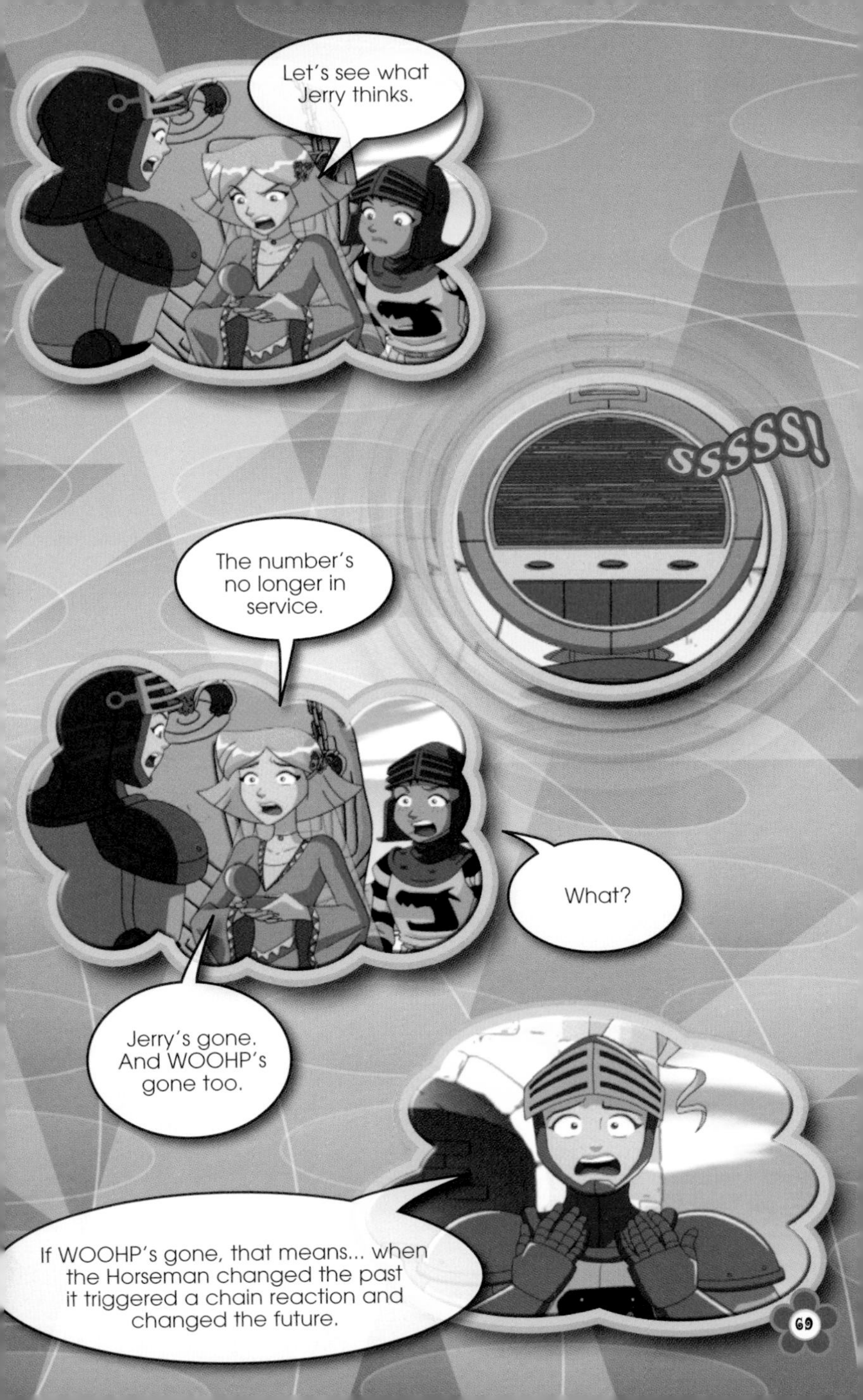
Let's see what Jerry thinks.
SSSSS!
The number's no longer in service.
What?
Jerry's gone. And WOOHP's gone too.
If WOOHP's gone, that means... when the Horseman changed the past it triggered a chain reaction and changed the future.

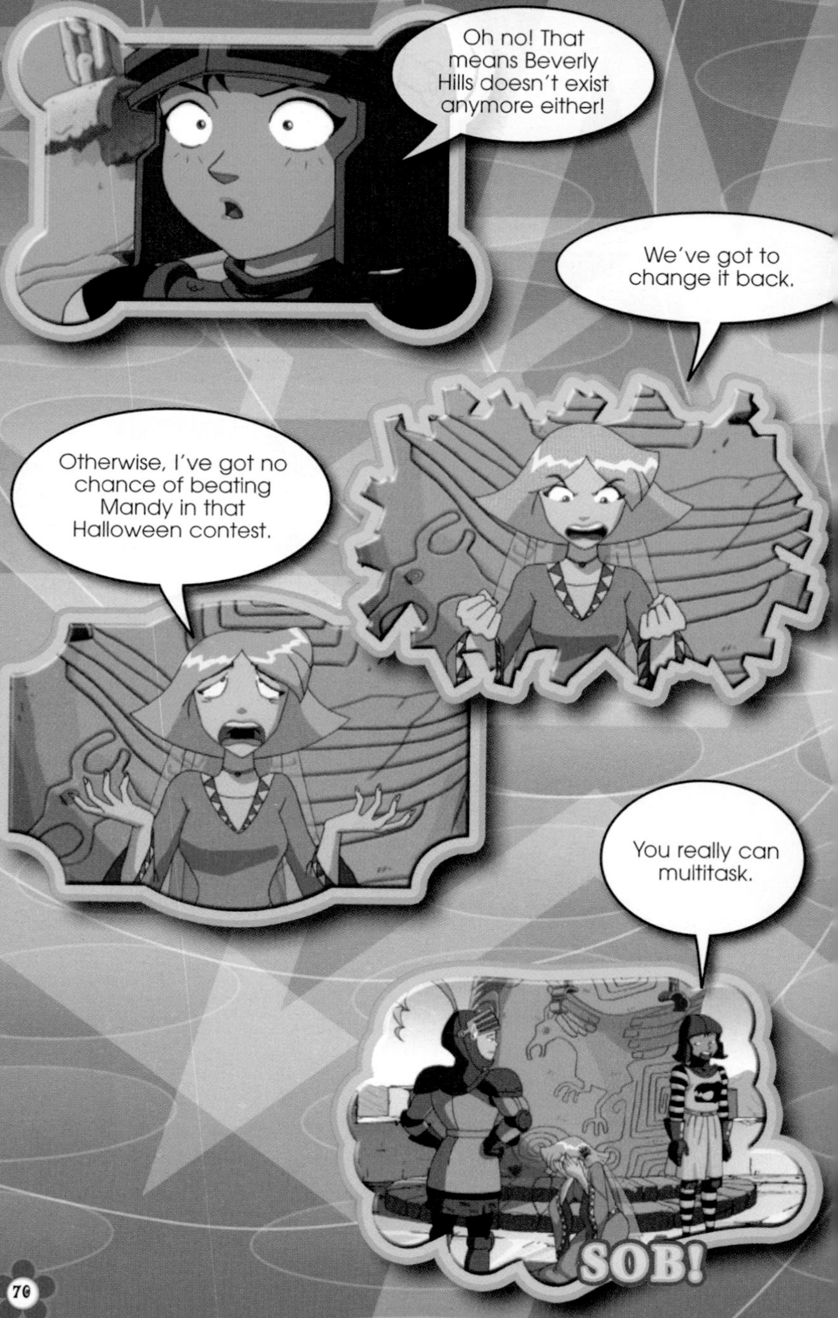
Oh no! That means Beverly Hills doesn't exist anymore either!
We've got to change it back.
Otherwise, I've got no chance of beating Mandy in that Halloween contest.
You really can multitask.
SOB!

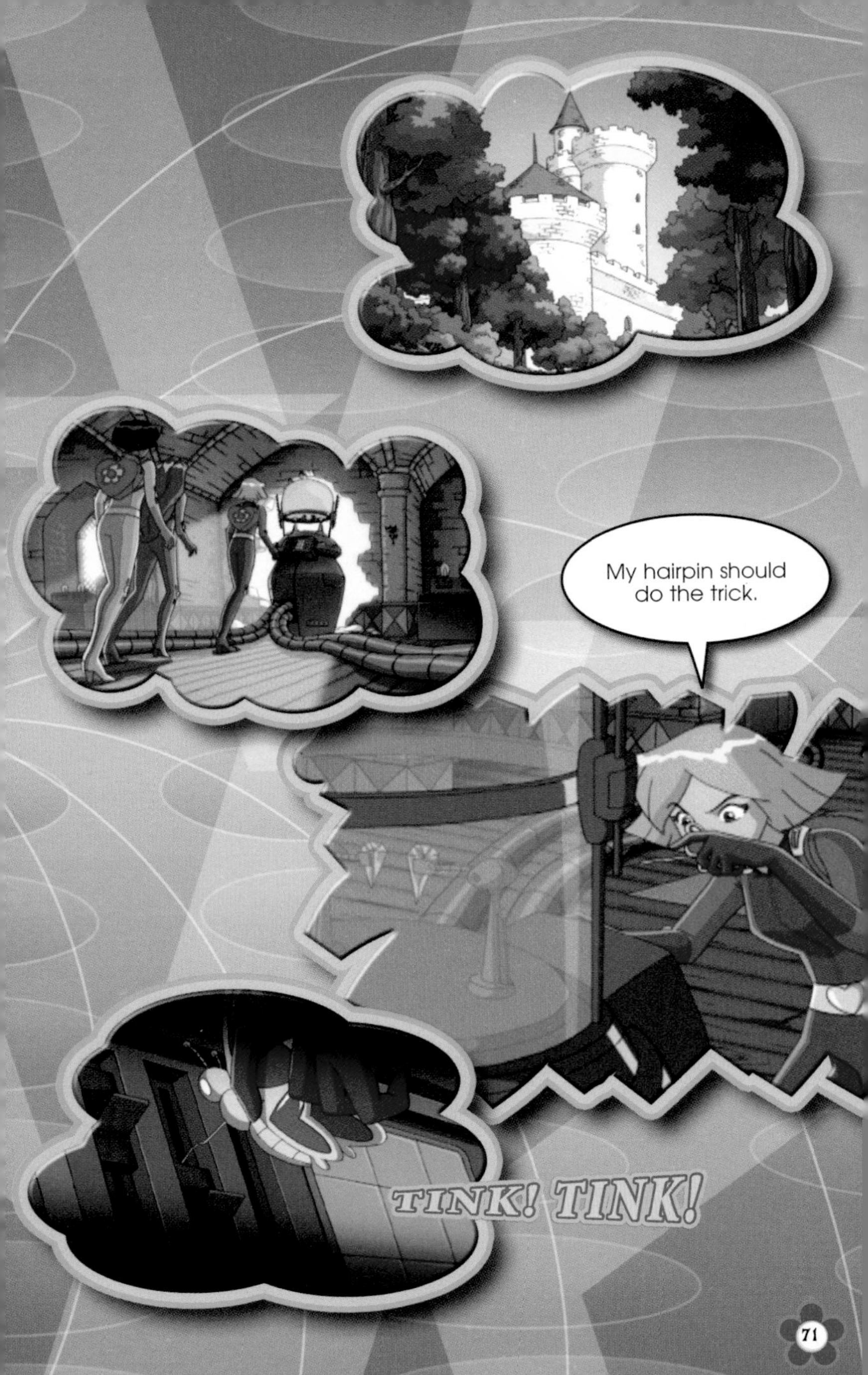
My hairpin should do the trick.
TINK! TINK!

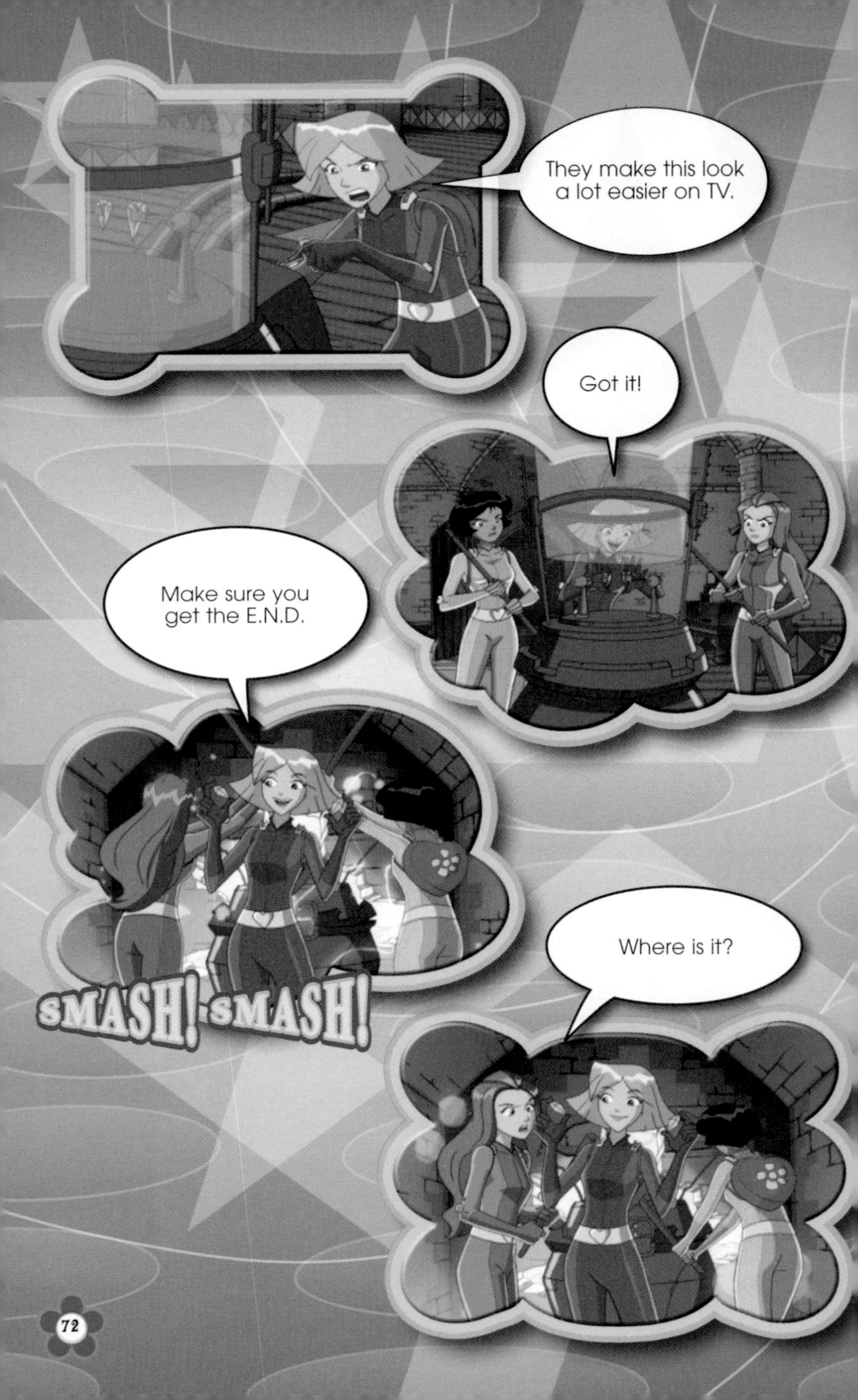
They make this look a lot easier on TV.
Got it!
Make sure you get the E.N.D.
SMASH! SMASH!
Where is it?

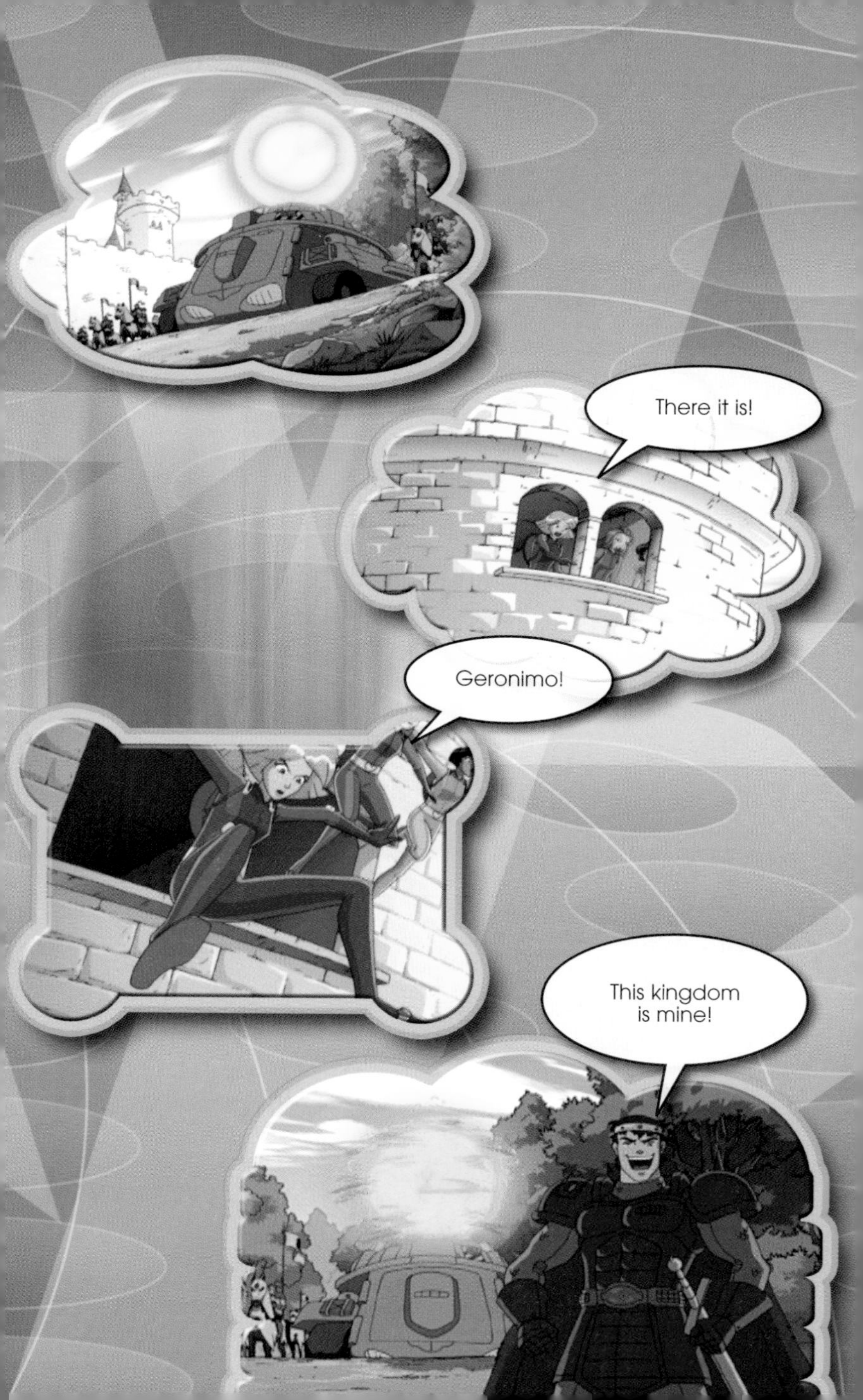
There it is!
Geronimo!
This kingdom is mine!

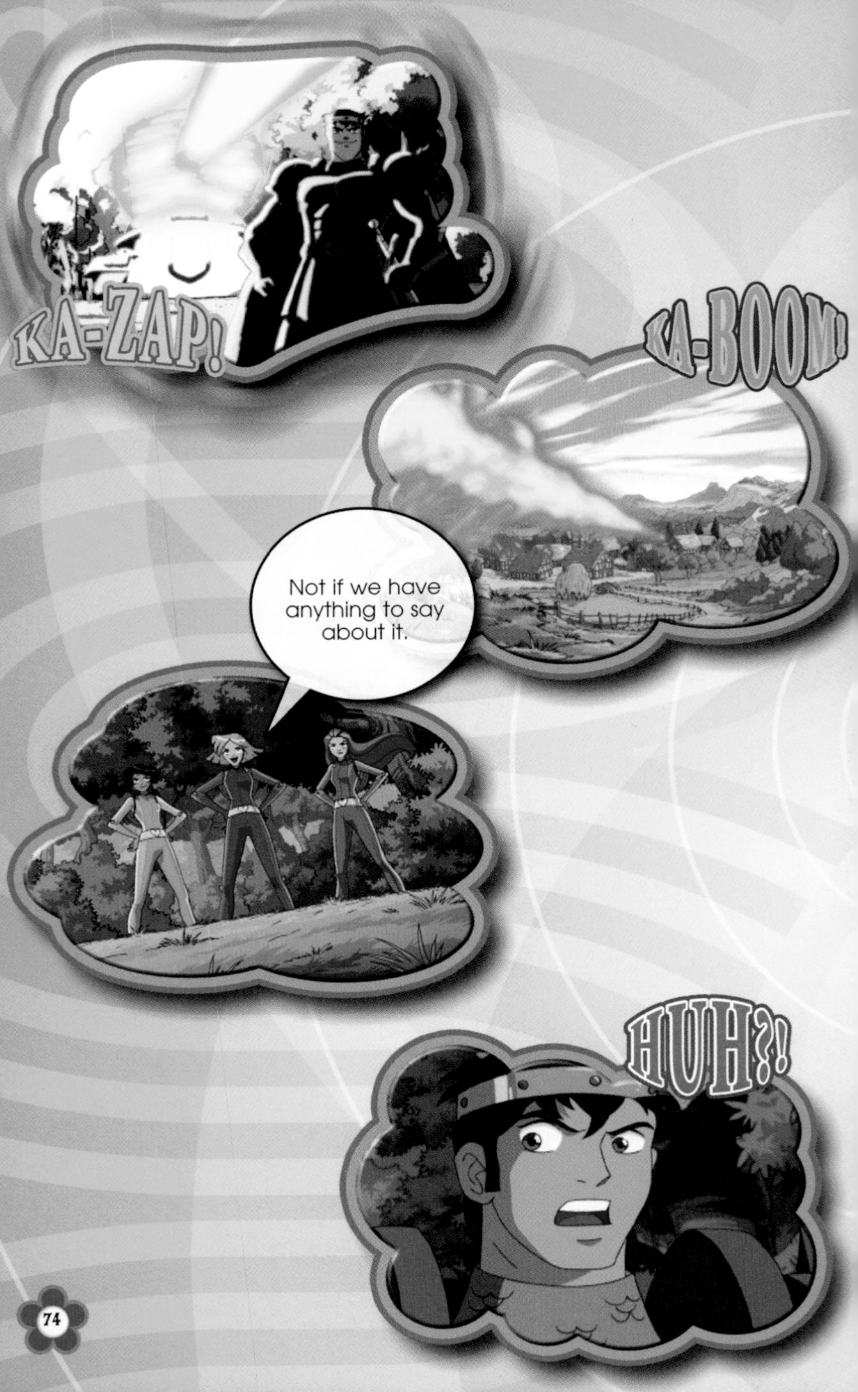
KA-ZAP!
KA-BOOM!
Not if we have anything to say about it.
HUH?!

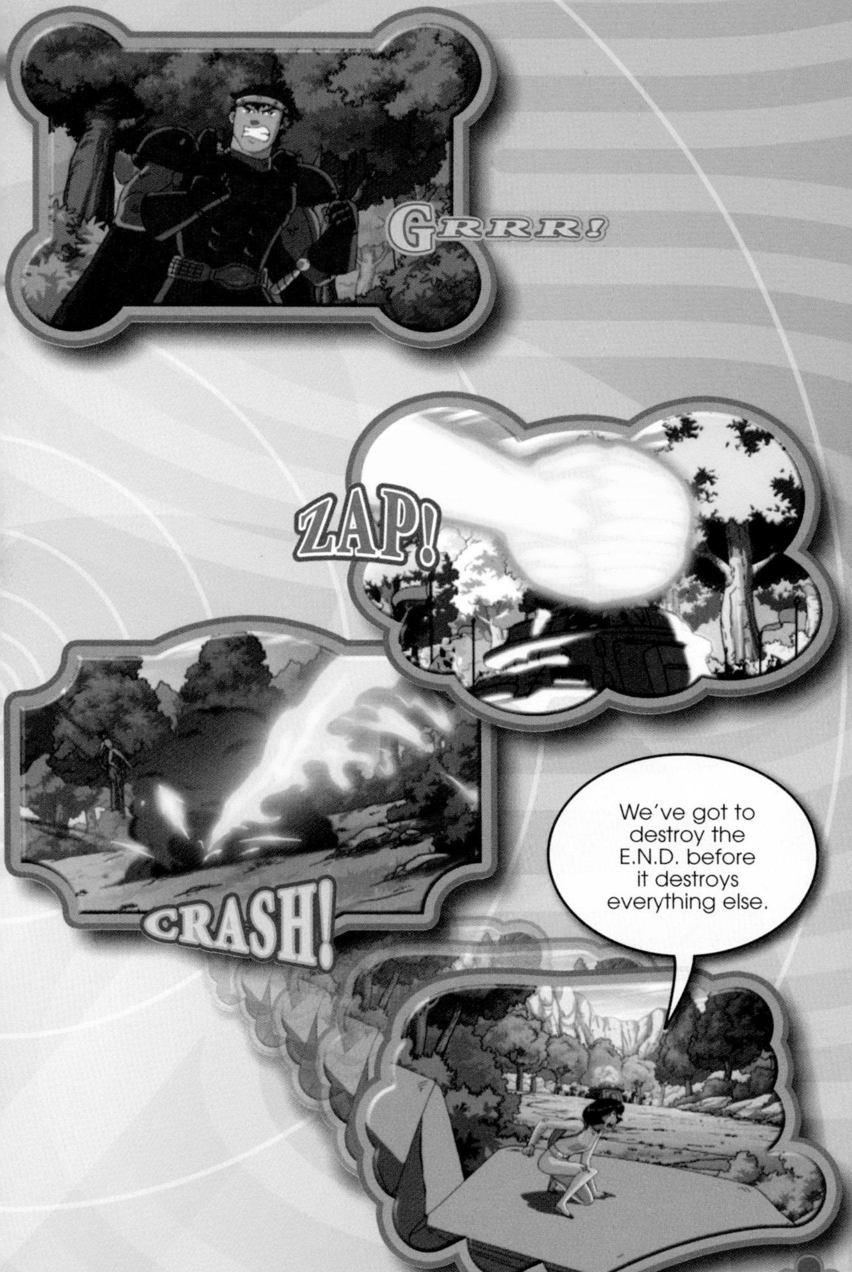
GRRR!
ZAP!
CRASH!
We've got to destroy the E.N.D. before it destroys everything else.

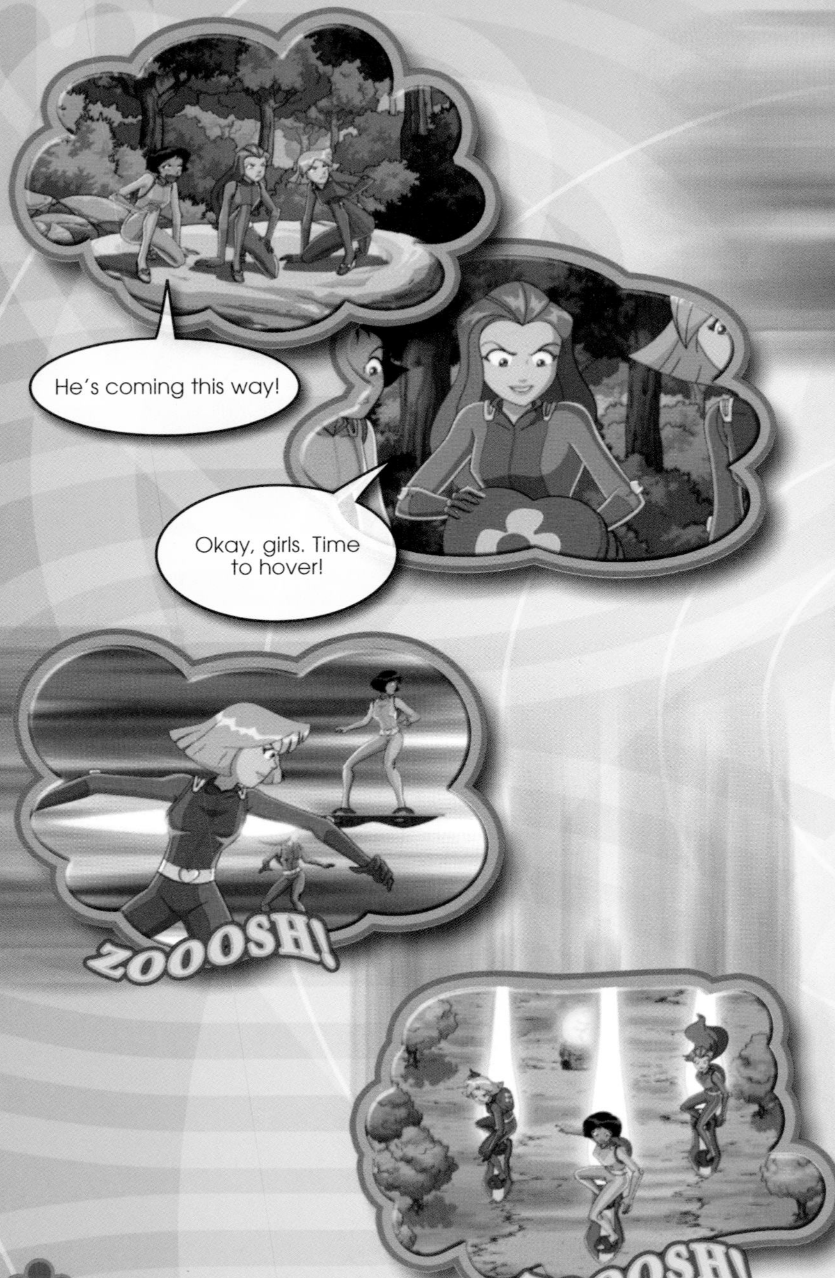
He's coming this way!
Okay, girls. Time to hover!
ZOOOSH!
ZOOOSH!

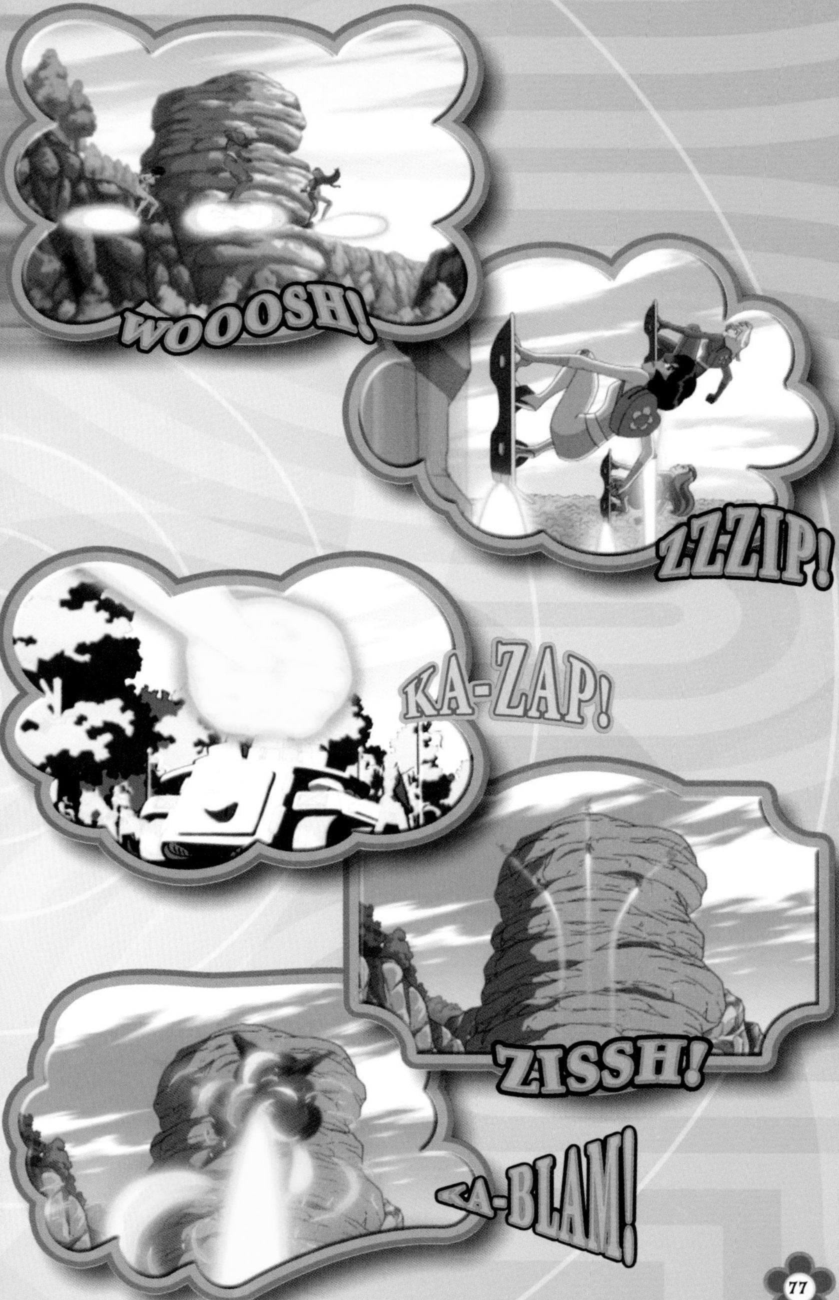
WOOOSH!
ZZZIP!
KA-ZAP!
ZISSH!
KA-BLAM!

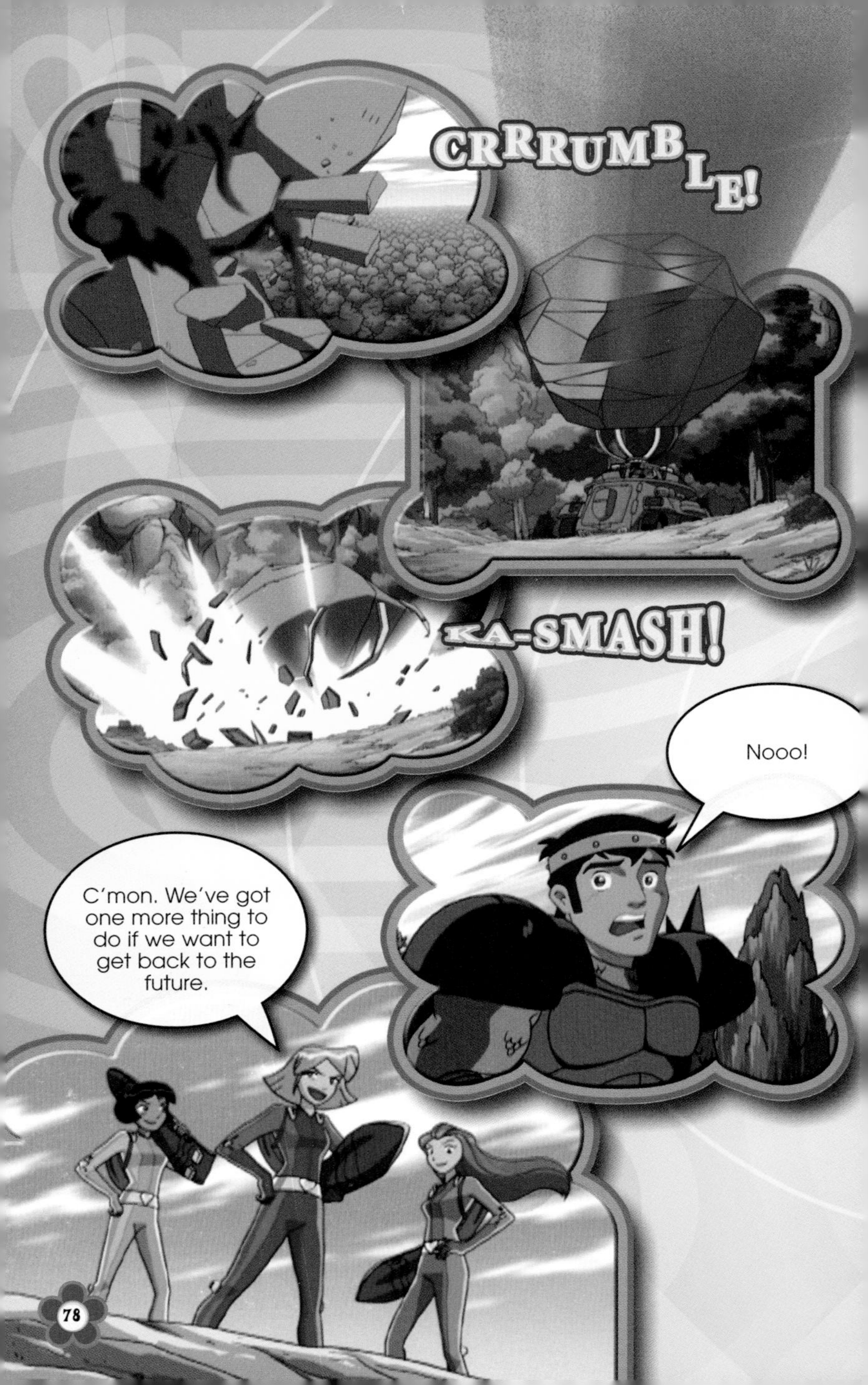
CRRRUMBLE!
KA-SMASH!
Nooo!
C'mon. We've got one more thing to do if we want to get back to the future.

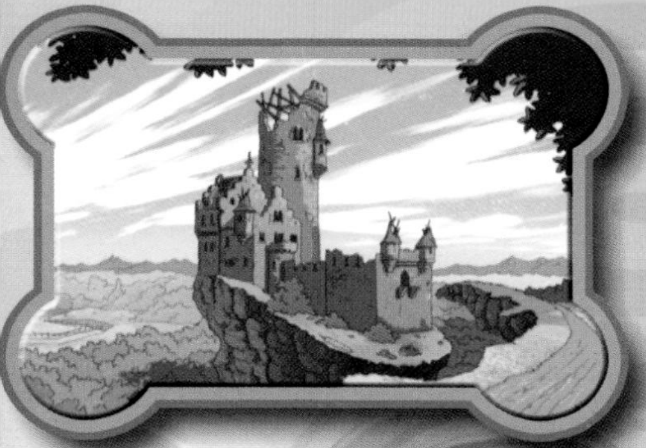

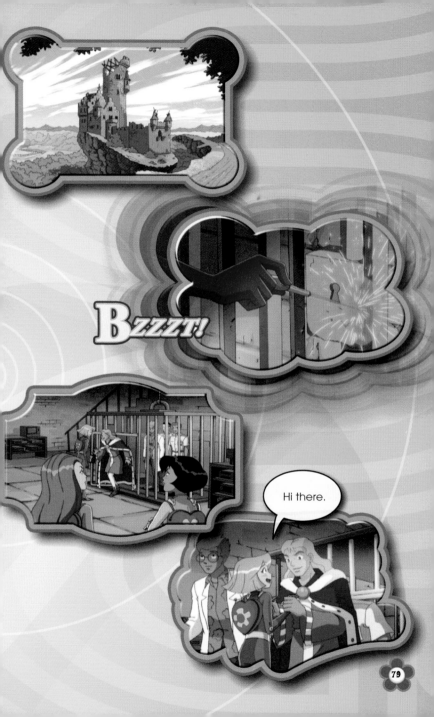

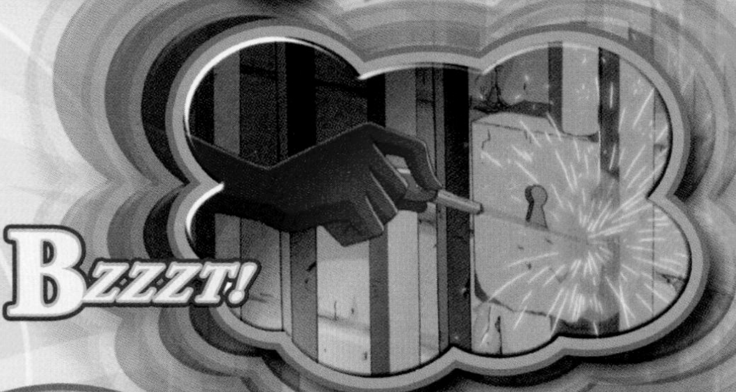
Bzzzt!

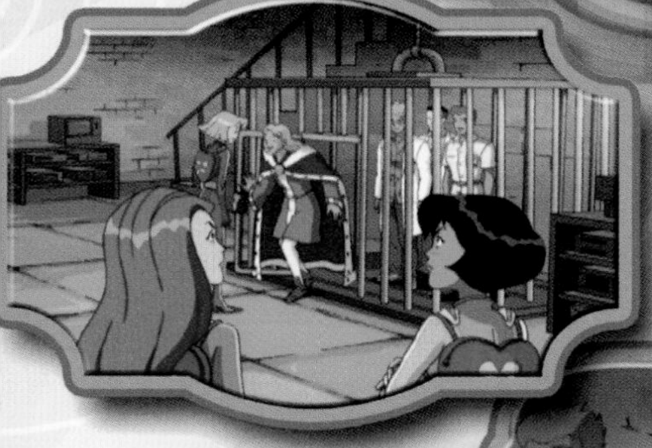

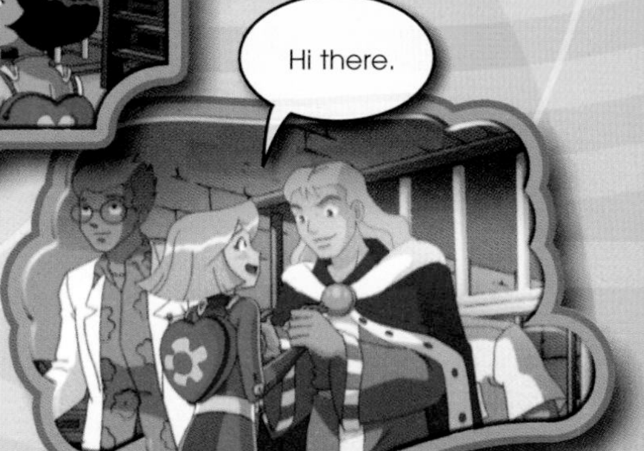
Hi there.

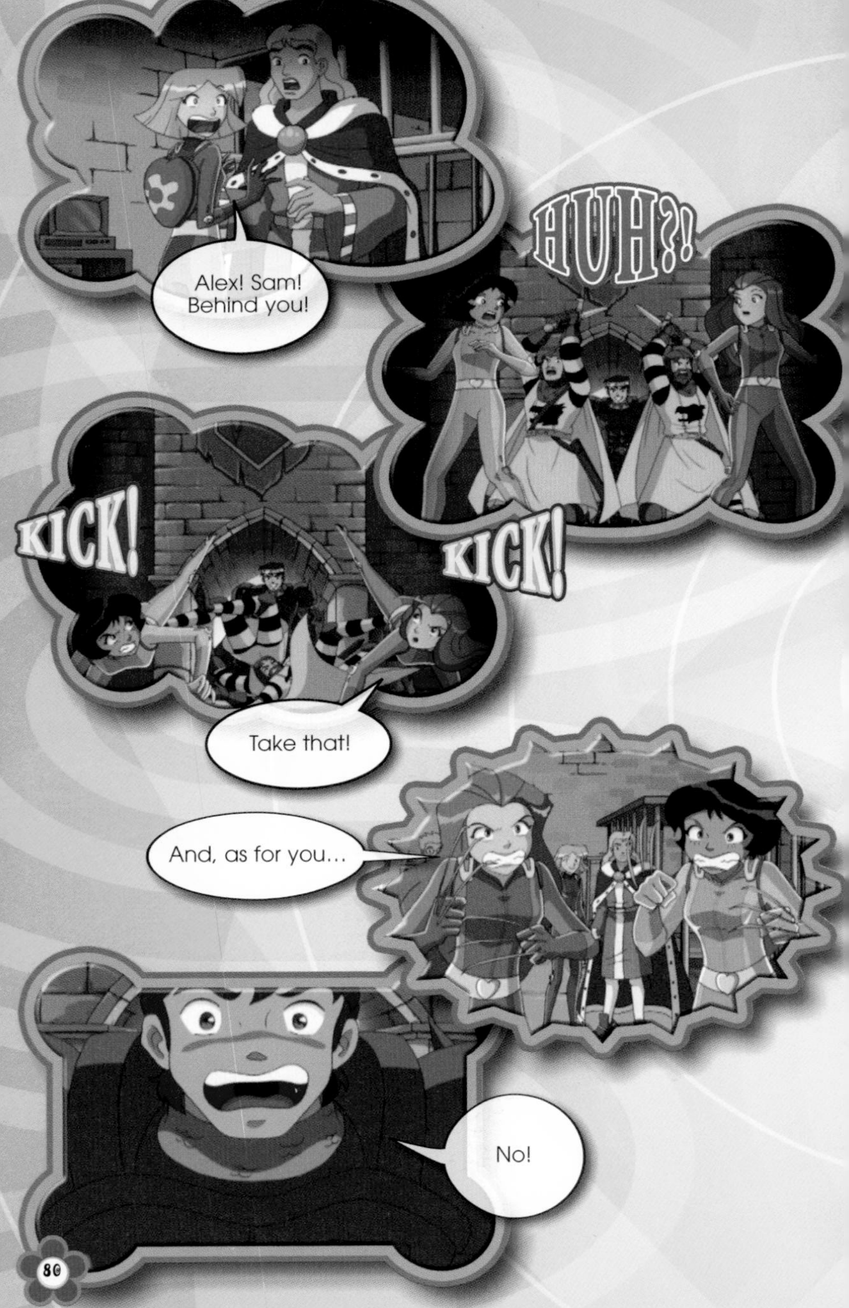
Alex! Sam!
Behind you!
HUH?!
KICK!
KICK!
Take that!
And, as for you...
No!

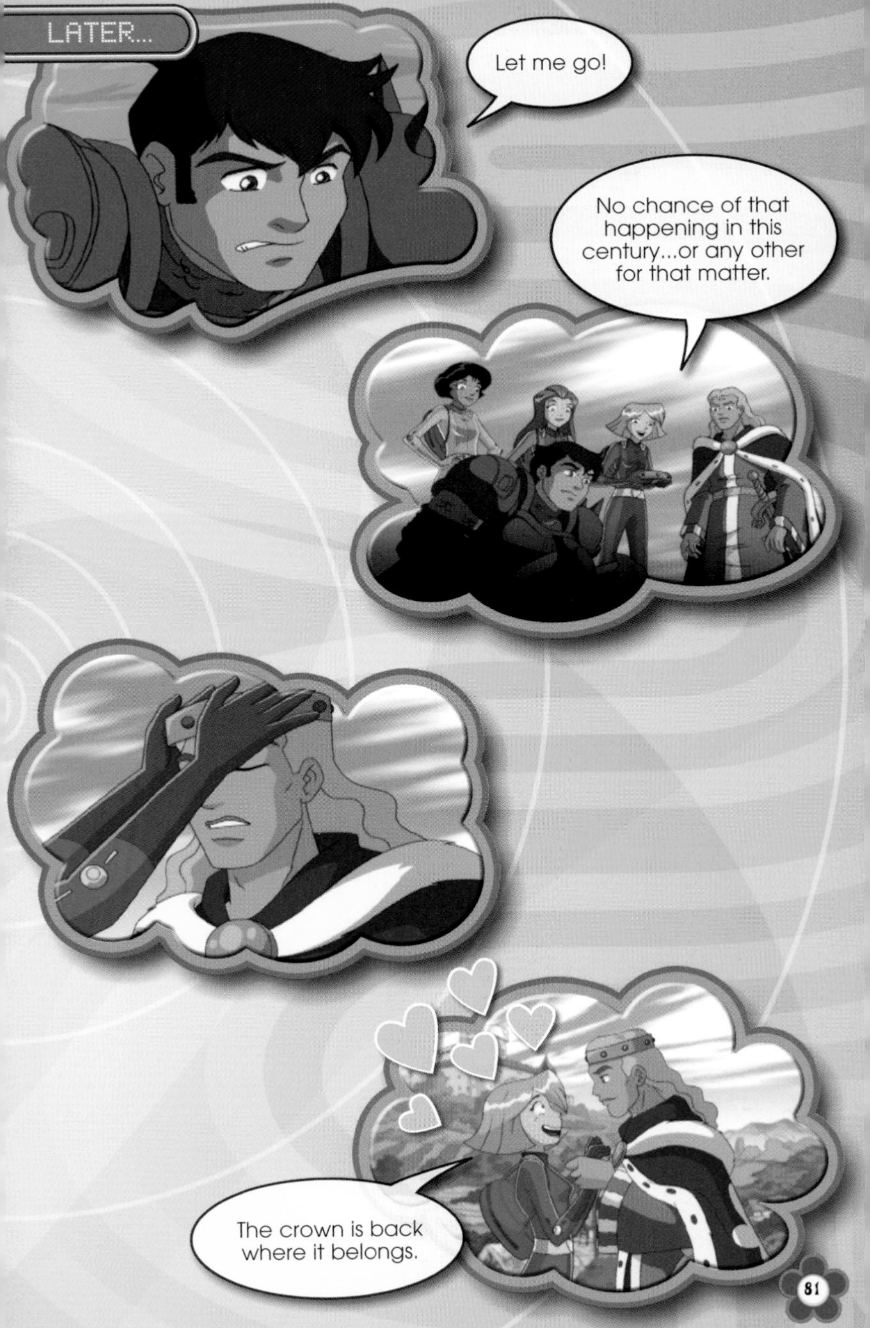
LATER...
Let me go!
No chance of that happening in this century...or any other for that matter.
The crown is back where it belongs.

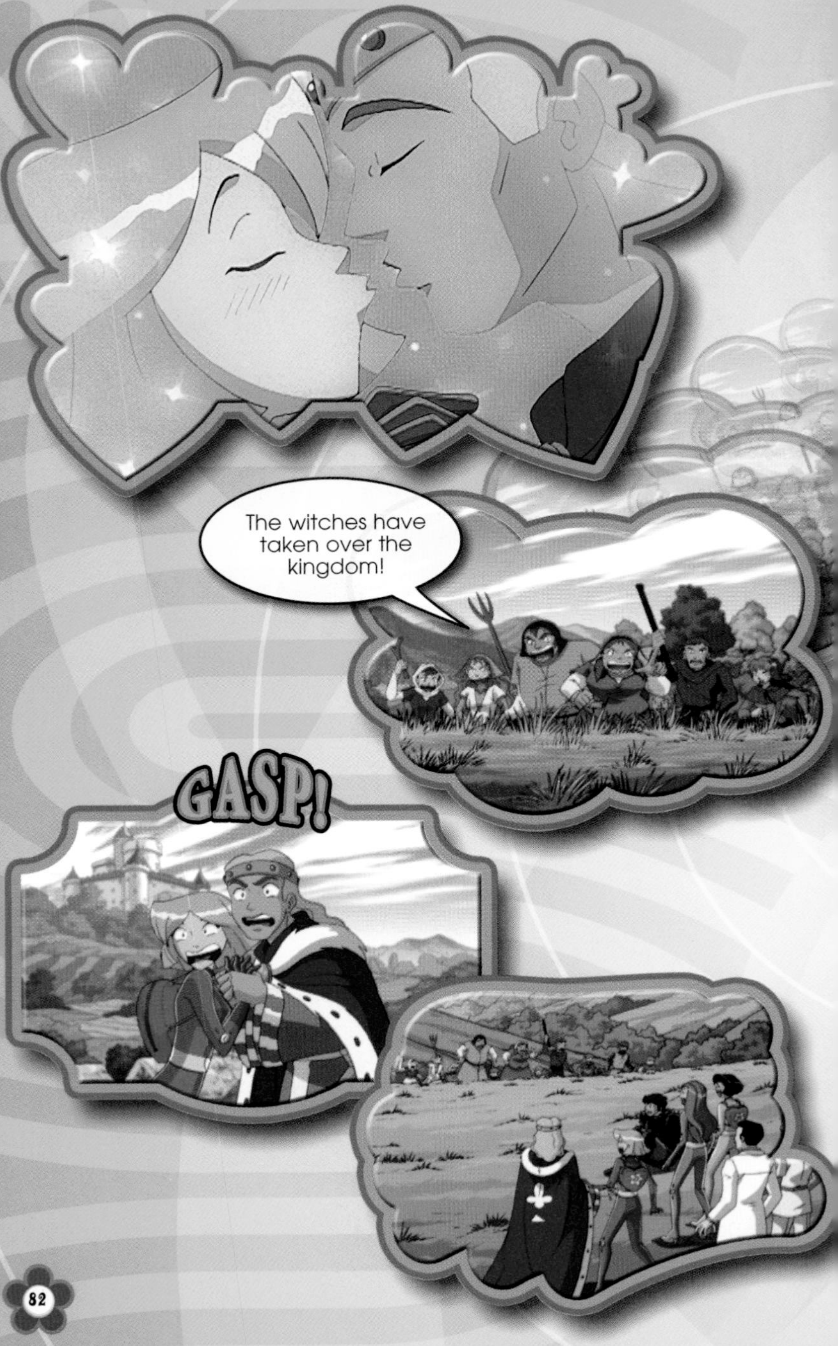
The witches have taken over the kingdom!
GASP!

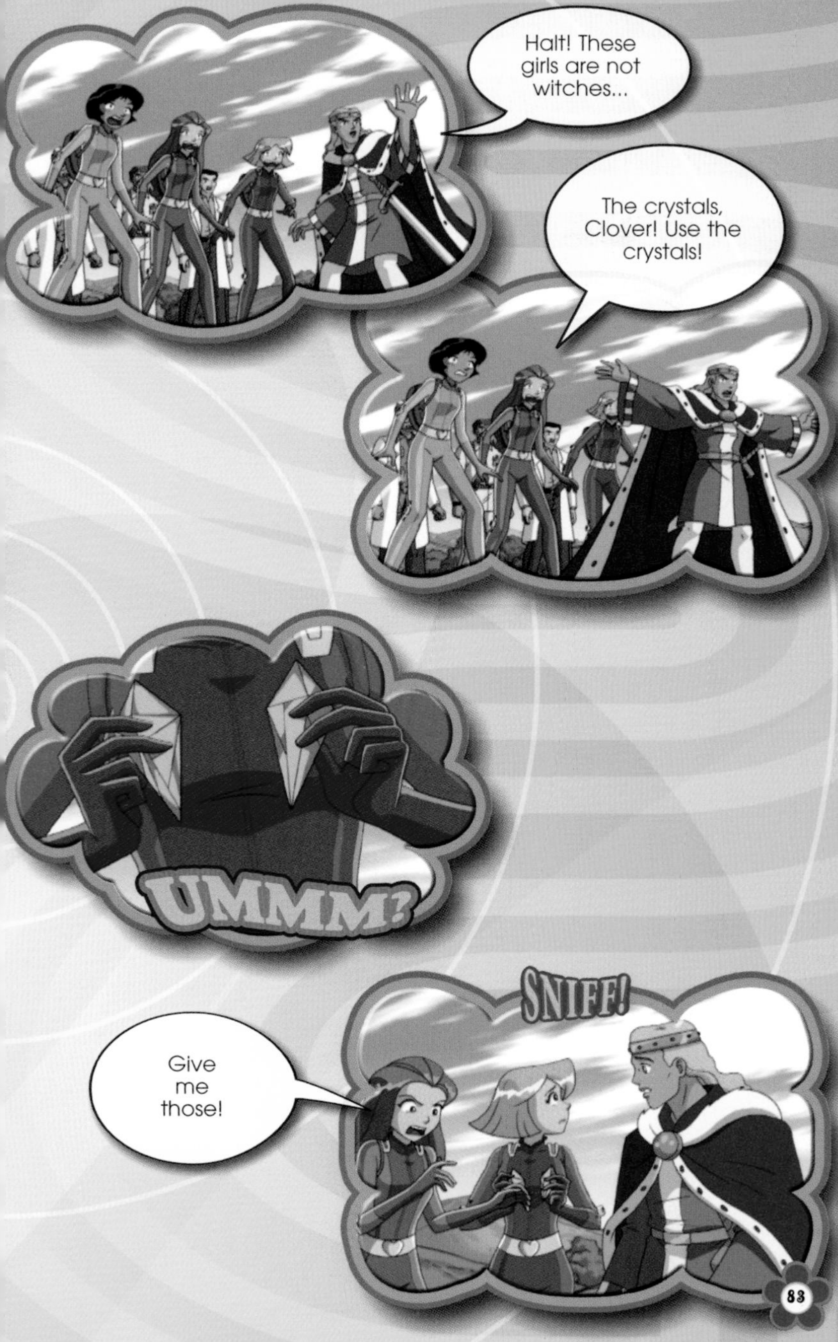
Halt! These girls are not witches...
The crystals, Clover! Use the crystals!
UMMM?
SNIFF!
Give me those!

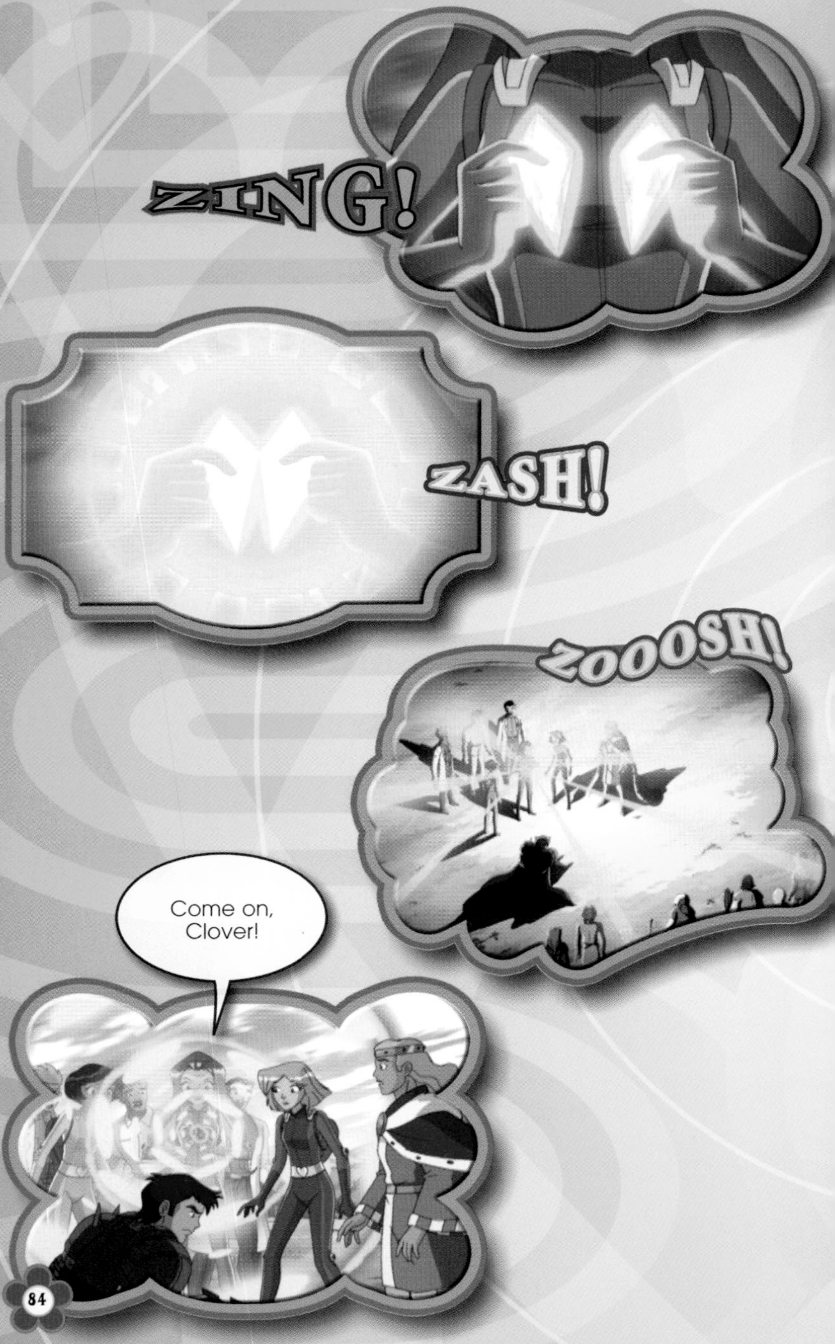
ZING!
ZASH!
ZOOOSH!
Come on, Clover!

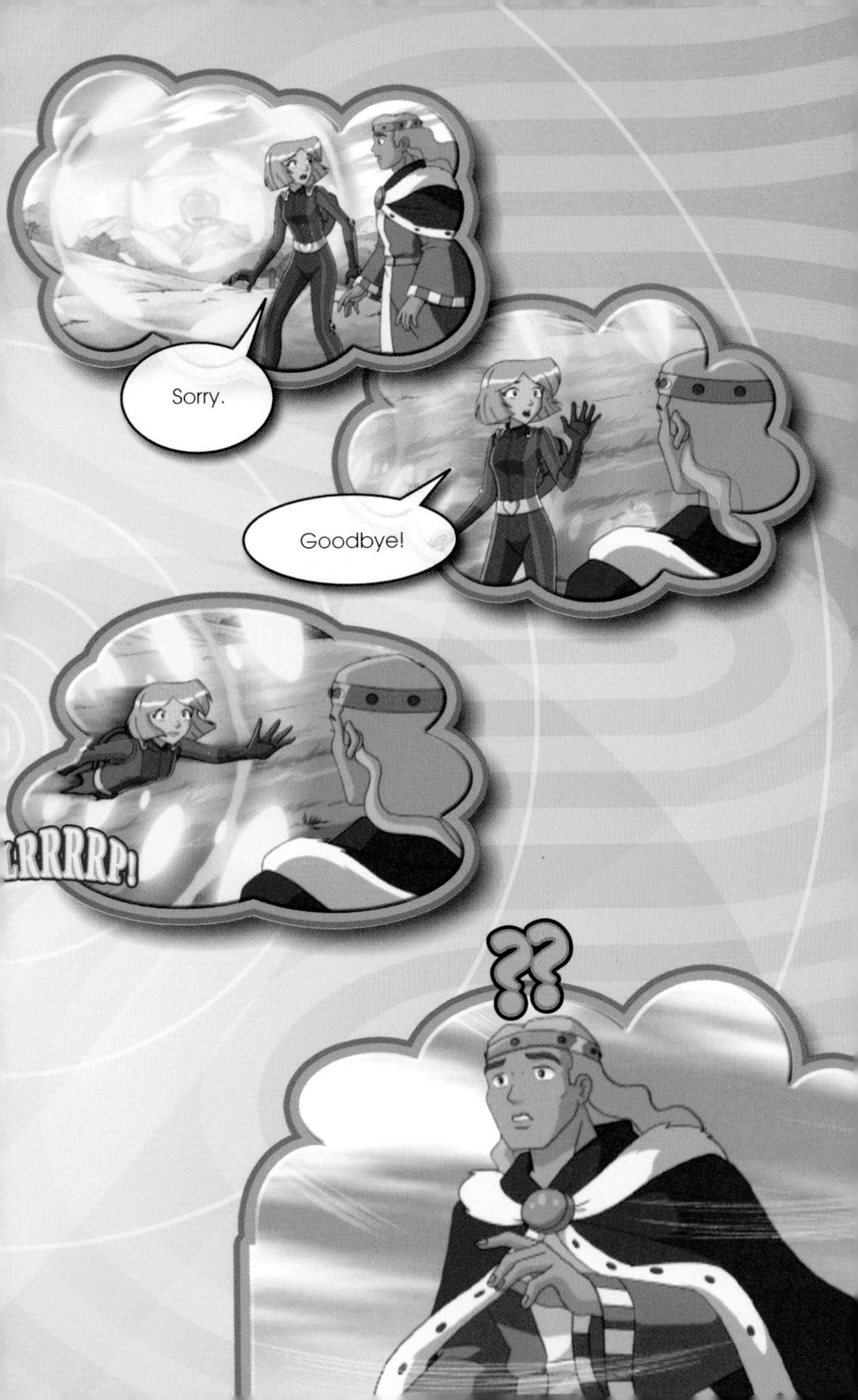
Sorry.
Goodbye!
RRRRP!
??

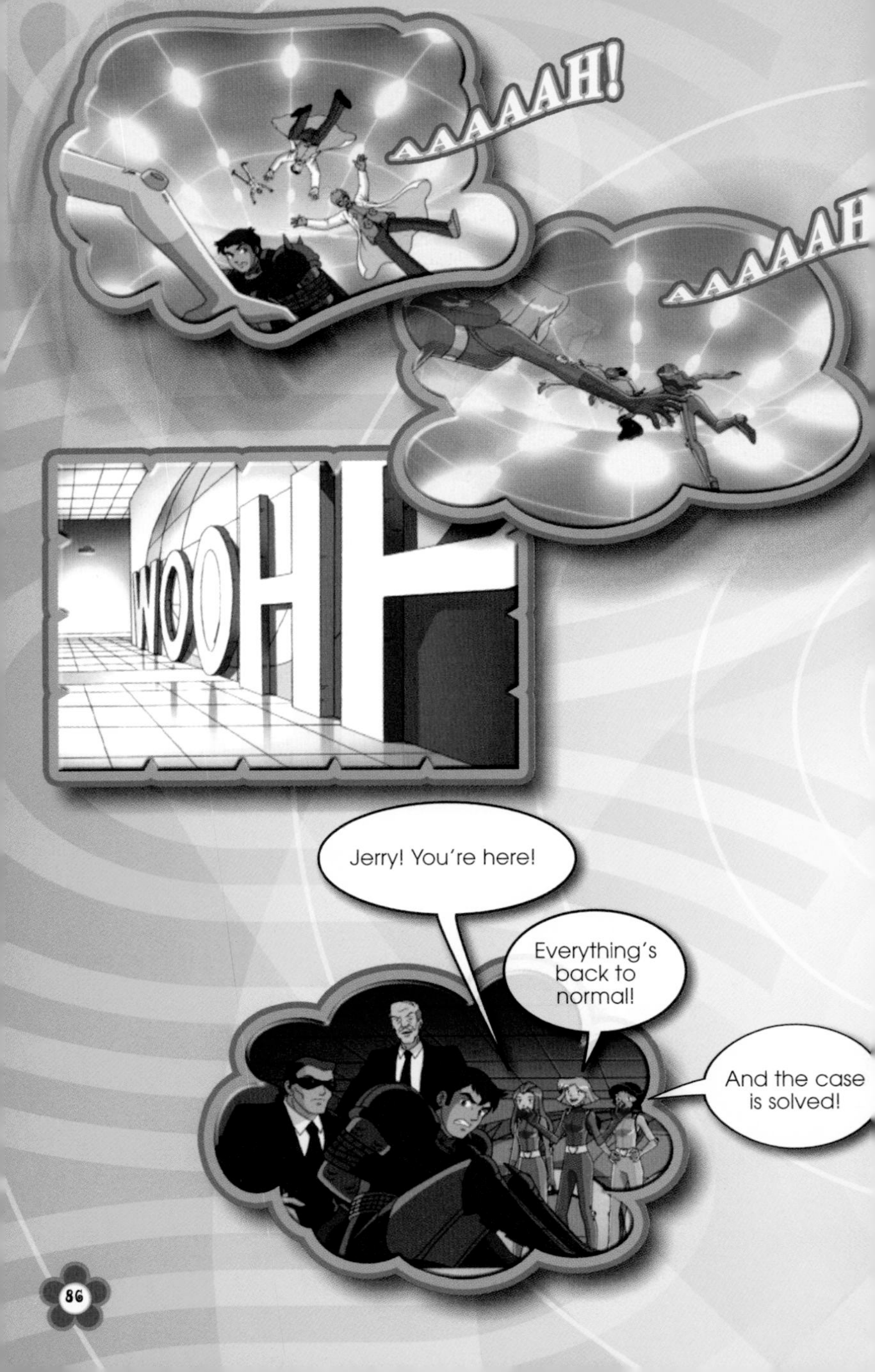
AAAAAH!
Jerry! You're here!
Everything's back to normal!
And the case is solved!

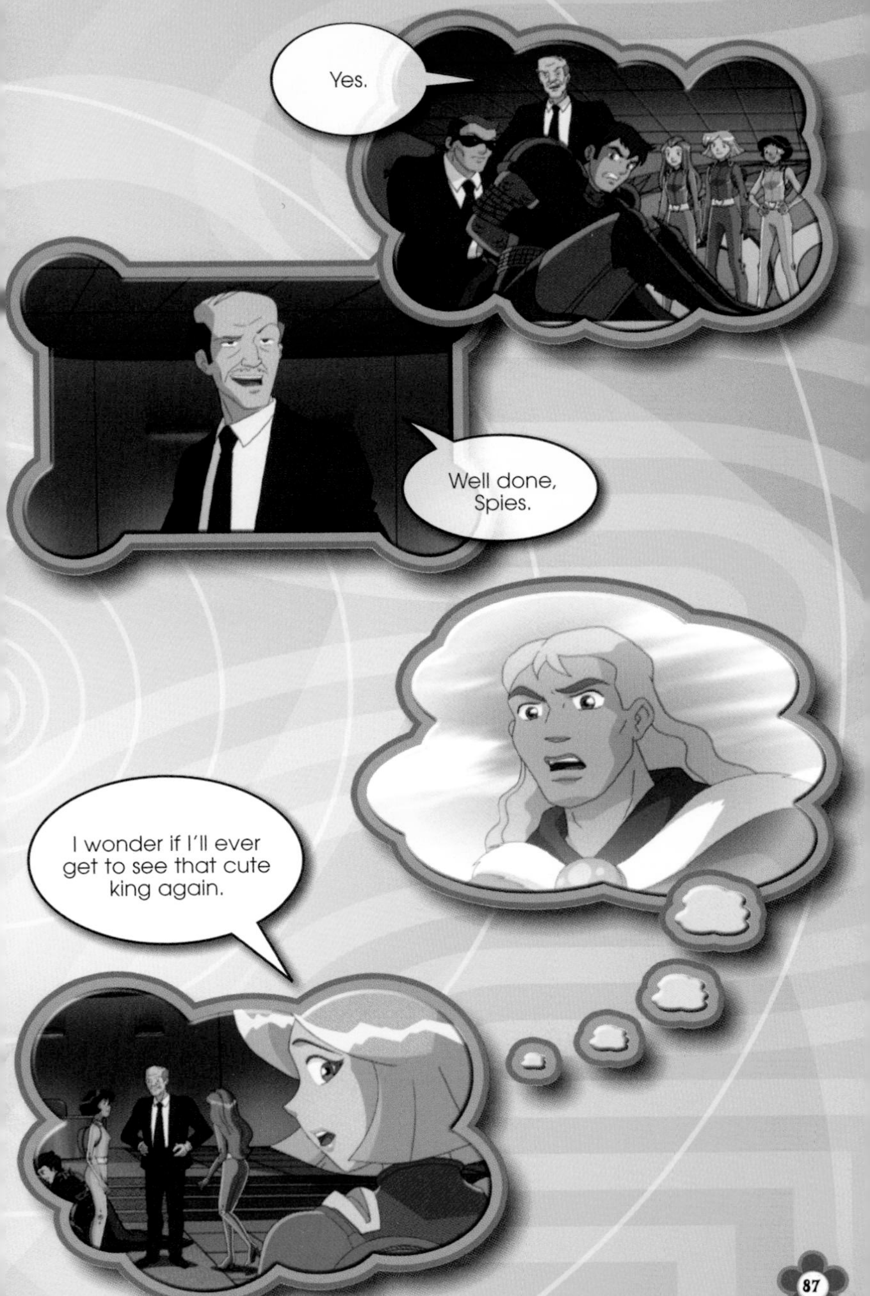
Yes.
Well done, Spies.
I wonder if I'll ever get to see that cute king again.

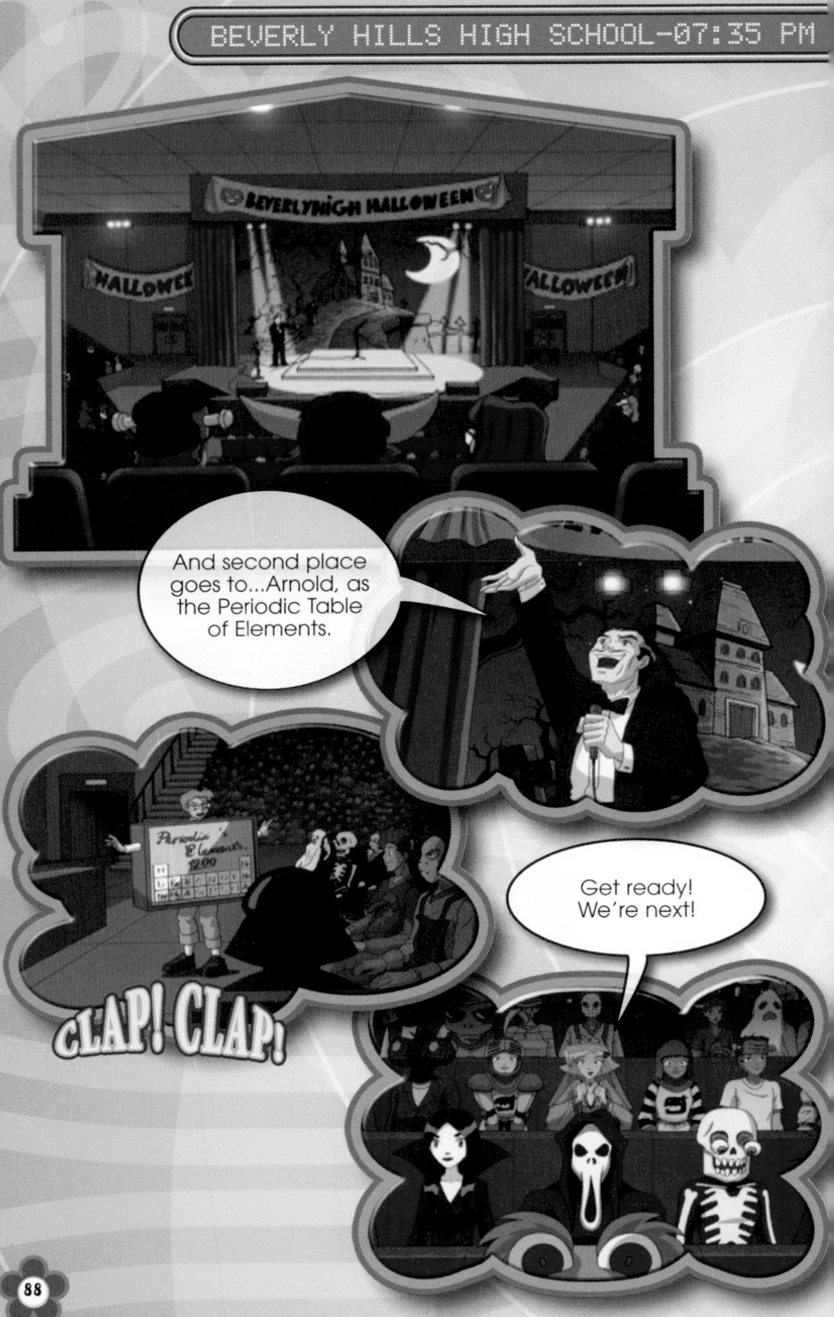
BEVERLY HILLS HIGH SCHOOL-07:35 PM
BEVERLYHIGH HALLOWEEN
And second place goes to...Arnold, as the Periodic Table of Elements.
CLAP! CLAP!
Get ready! We're next!

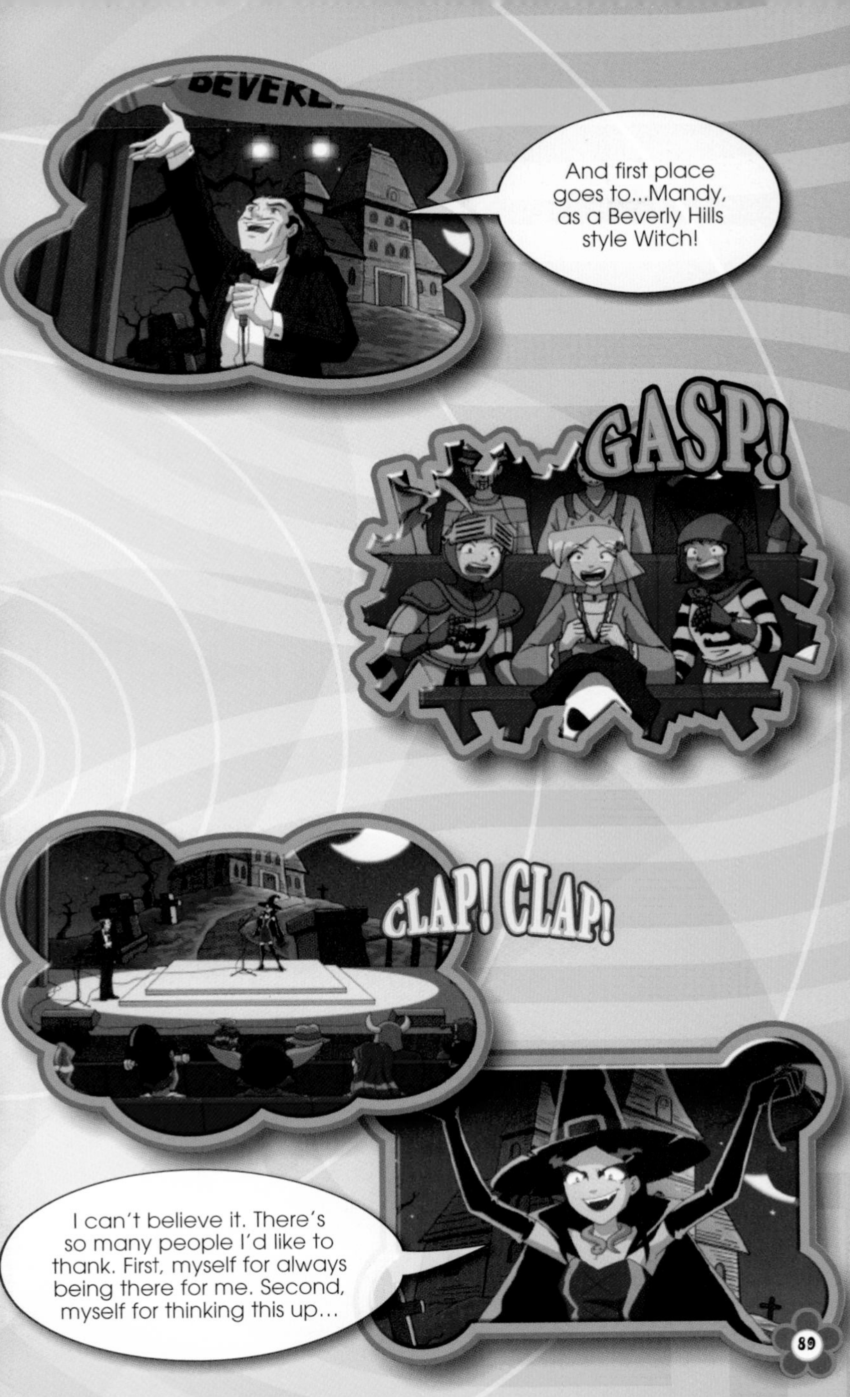
And first place goes to...Mandy, as a Beverly Hills style Witch!
GASP!
CLAP! CLAP!
I can't believe it. There's so many people I'd like to thank. First, myself for always being there for me. Second, myself for thinking this up…

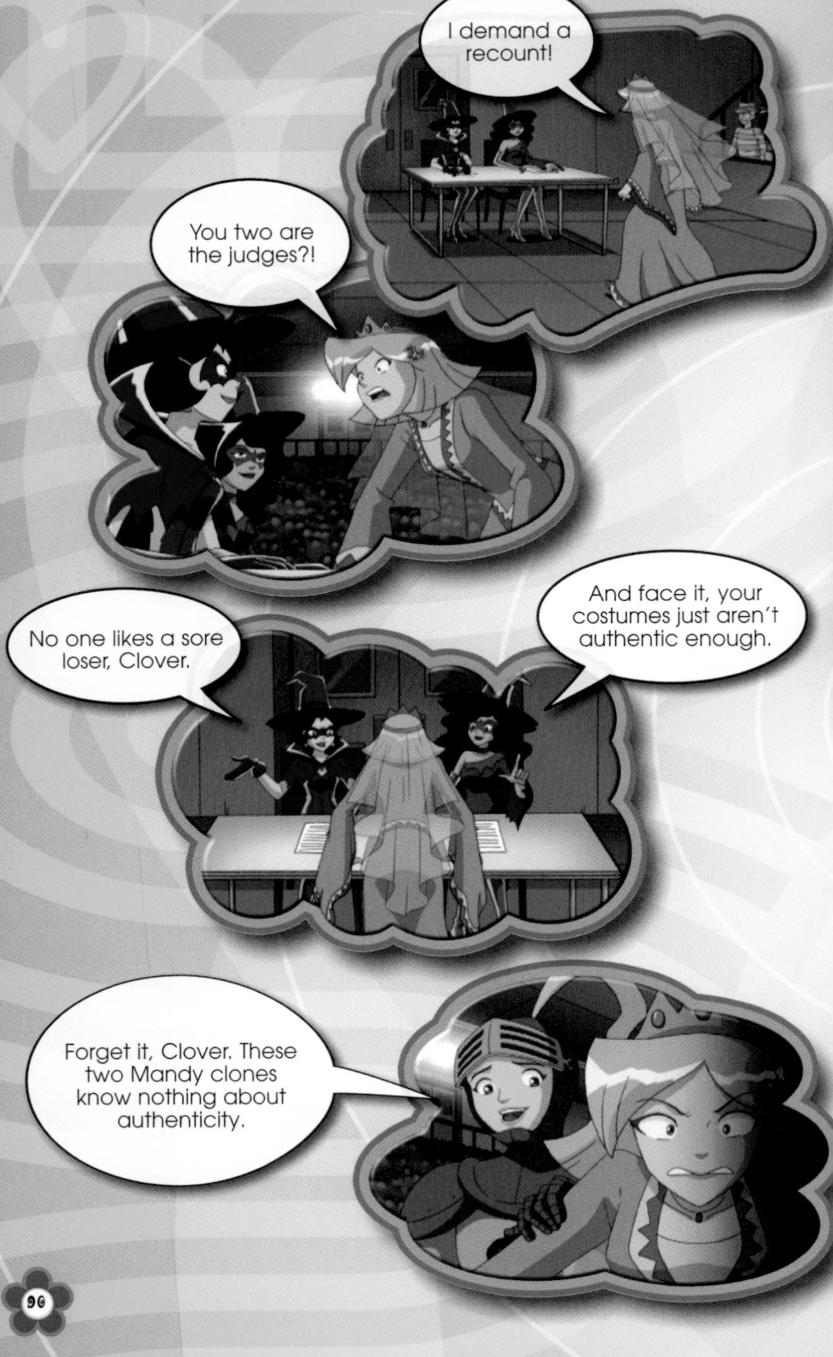
I demand a recount!
You two are the judges?!
No one likes a sore loser, Clover.
And face it, your costumes just aren't authentic enough.
Forget it, Clover. These two Mandy clones know nothing about authenticity.

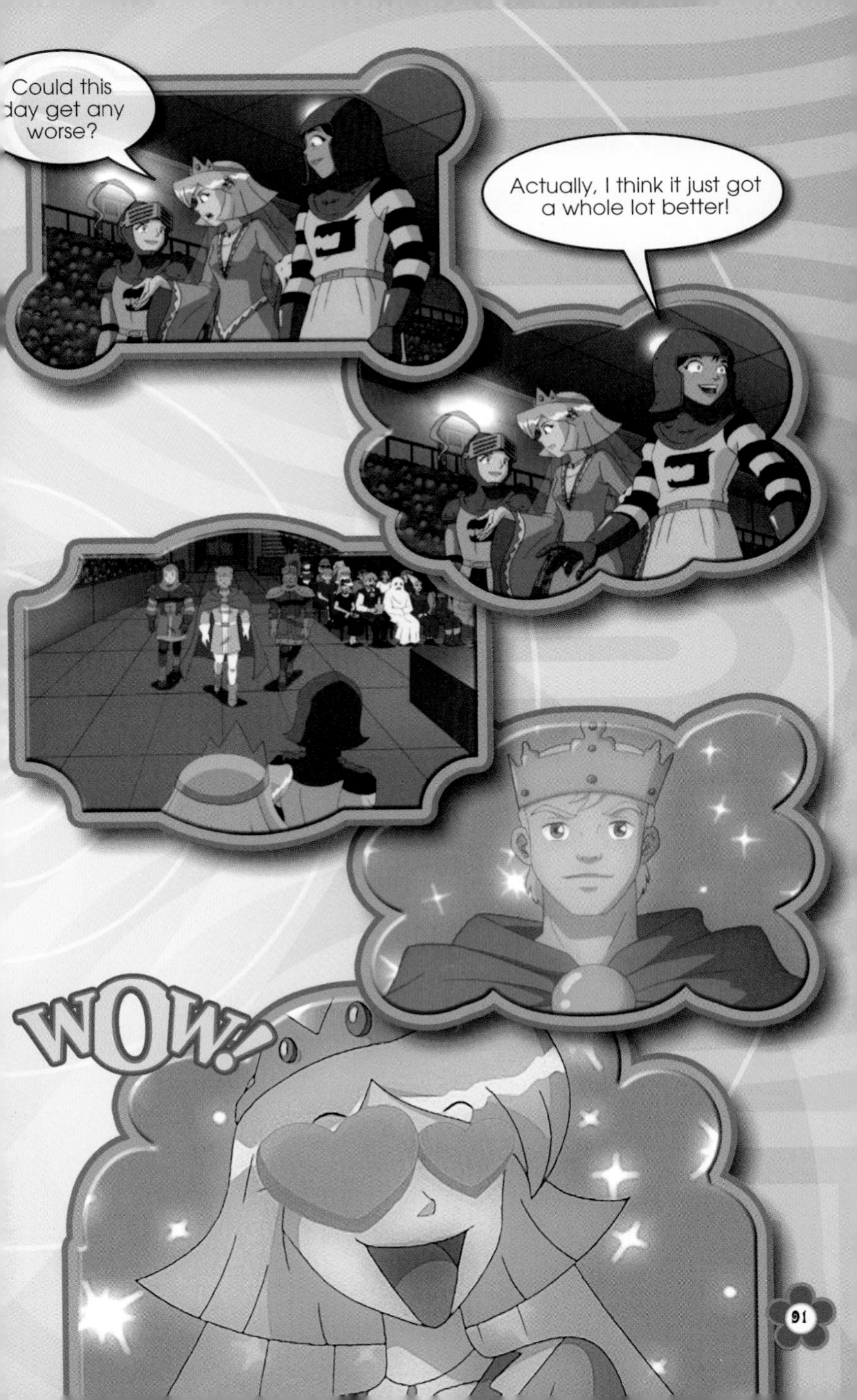
Could this
day get any
worse?
Actually, I think it just got
a whole lot better!
WOW!

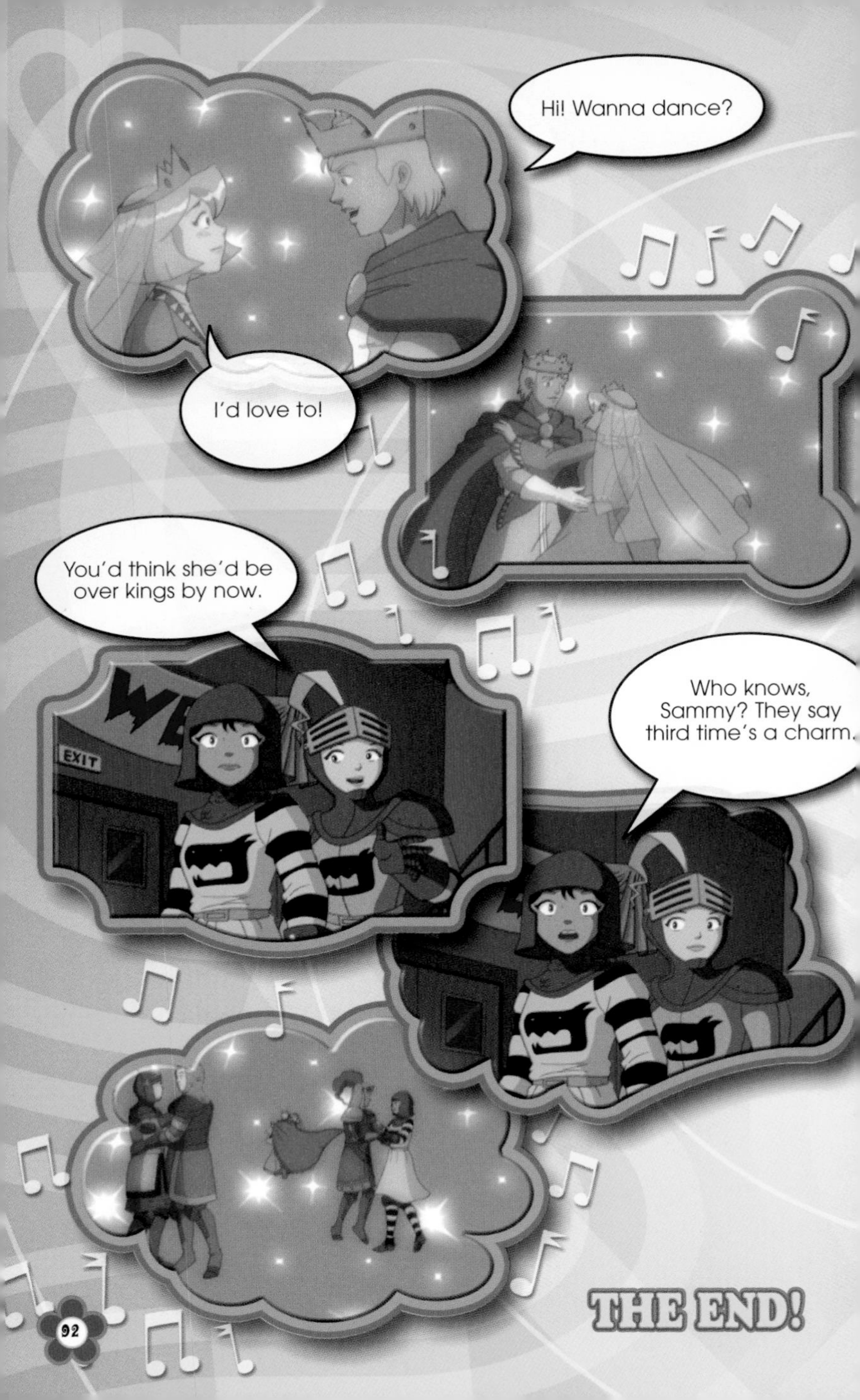
Hi! Wanna dance?
I'd love to!
You'd think she'd be over kings by now.
Who knows, Sammy? They say third time's a charm.
EXIT
THE END!

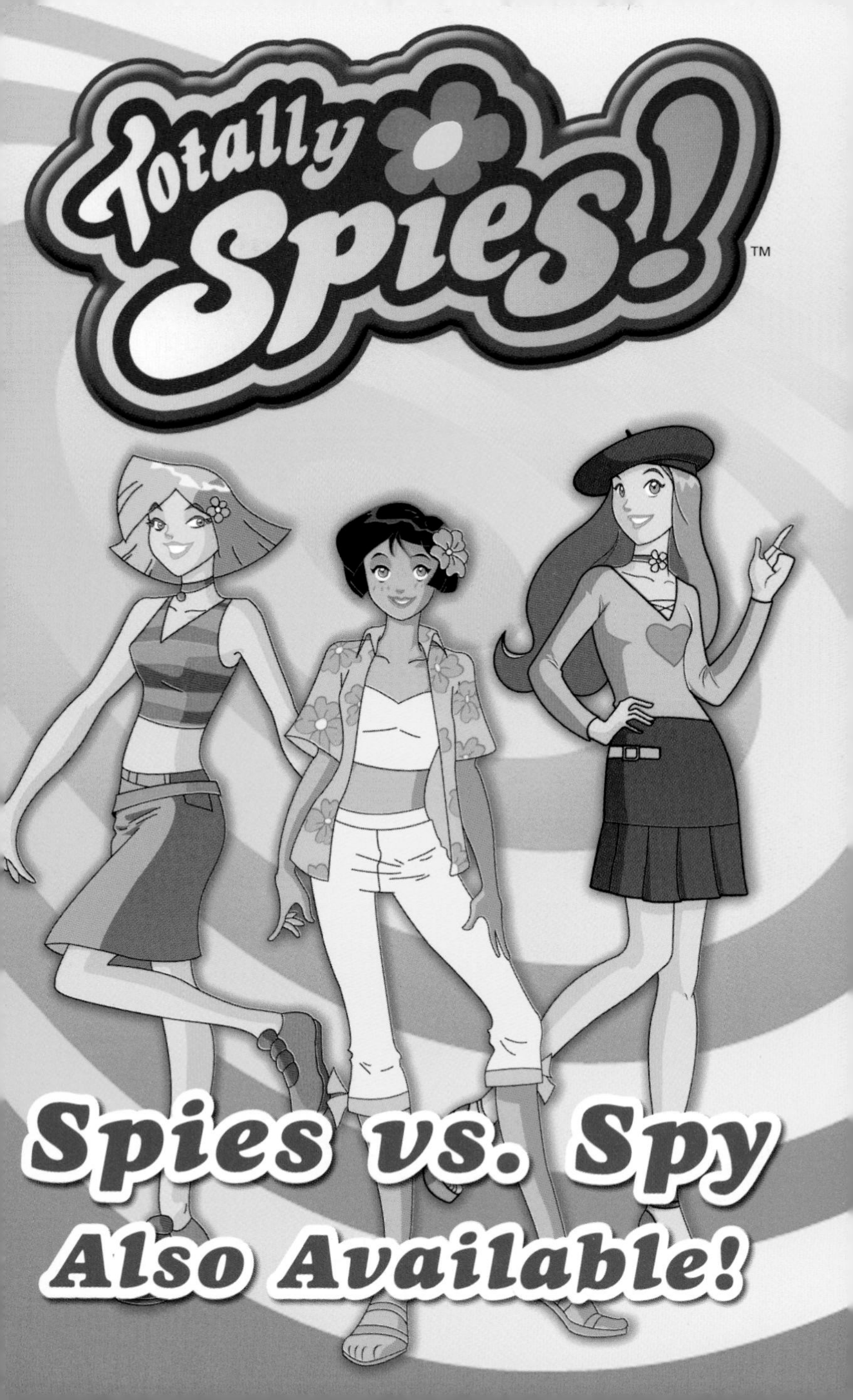
Totally Spies!™
Spies vs. Spy
Also Available!

MANGA

.HACK//LEGEND OF THE TWILIGHT
ALICHINO
ANGELIC LAYER
BABY BIRTH
BRAIN POWERED
BRIGADOON
B'TX
CANDIDATE FOR GODDESS, THE
CARDCAPTOR SAKURA
CARDCAPTOR SAKURA - MASTER OF THE CLOW
CHRONICLES OF THE CURSED SWORD
CLAMP SCHOOL DETECTIVES
CLOVER
COMIC PARTY
CORRECTOR YUI
COWBOY BEBOP
COWBOY BEBOP: SHOOTING STAR
CRESCENT MOON
CROSS
CULDCEPT
CYBORG 009
D•N•ANGEL
DEARS
DEMON DIARY
DEMON ORORON, THE
DIGIMON
DIGIMON TAMERS
DIGIMON ZERO TWO
DRAGON HUNTER
DRAGON KNIGHTS
DRAGON VOICE
DREAM SAGA
DUKLYON: CLAMP SCHOOL DEFENDERS
ET CETERA
ETERNITY
FAERIES' LANDING
FLCL
FLOWER OF THE DEEP SLEEP
FORBIDDEN DANCE
FRUITS BASKET
G GUNDAM
GATEKEEPERS
GIRL GOT GAME
GUNDAM SEED ASTRAY
GUNDAM WING
GUNDAM WING: BATTLEFIELD OF PACIFISTS
GUNDAM WING: ENDLESS WALTZ
GUNDAM WING: THE LAST OUTPOST (G-UNIT)
HANDS OFF!

HARLEM BEAT
HYPER RUNE
I.N.V.U.
INITIAL D
INSTANT TEEN: JUST ADD NUTS
JING: KING OF BANDITS
JING: KING OF BANDITS - TWILIGHT TALES
JULINE
KARE KANO
KILL ME, KISS ME
KINDAICHI CASE FILES, THE
KING OF HELL
KODOCHA: SANA'S STAGE
LEGEND OF CHUN HYANG, THE
LOVE OR MONEY
MAGIC KNIGHT RAYEARTH I
MAGIC KNIGHT RAYEARTH II
MAN OF MANY FACES
MARMALADE BOY
MARS
MARS: HORSE WITH NO NAME
MINK
MIRACLE GIRLS
MODEL
MOURYOU KIDEN: LEGEND OF THE NYMPH
NECK AND NECK
ONE
ONE I LOVE, THE
PEACH FUZZ
PEACH GIRL
PEACH GIRL: CHANGE OF HEART
PITA-TEN
PLANET LADDER
PLANETES
PRESIDENT DAD
PRINCESS AI
PSYCHIC ACADEMY
QUEEN'S KNIGHT, THE
RAGNAROK
RAVE MASTER
REALITY CHECK
REBIRTH
REBOUND
RISING STARS OF MANGA
SAILOR MOON
SAINT TAIL
SAMURAI GIRL REAL BOUT HIGH SCHOOL
SEIKAI TRILOGY, THE
SGT. FROG
SHAOLIN SISTERS

09

ALSO AVAILABLE FROM 🐾TOKYOPOP®